GENDER(S)

GENDER(S)

KATHRYN BOND STOCKTON

The MIT Press | Cambridge, Massachusetts | London, England

The MIT Press would like to thank the anonymous peer reviewers who provided comments on drafts of this book. The generous work of academic experts is essential for establishing the authority and quality of our publications. We acknowledge with gratitude the contributions of these otherwise uncredited readers.

The author warmly appreciates and acknowledges these venues that have published different versions of her ideas that appear in this book: *The Cambridge Companion to Gay and Lesbian Writing*; Oxford's *The Year's Work in Critical and Cultural Theory*; *NOVEL: A Forum on Fiction*; *WOMEN: A Cultural Review*; Duke University Press; and New York University Press.

This book was set in Chaparral Pro by New Best-set Typesetters Ltd. Printed and bound in the United States of America.

Library of Congress Cataloging-in-Publication Data

Names: Stockton, Kathryn Bond, 1958- author.
Title: Gender(s) / Kathryn Bond Stockton.
Description: Cambridge, Massachusetts : The MIT Press, [2021] | Series: The MIT Press essential knowledge series | Includes bibliographical references and index.
Identifiers: LCCN 2020040790 | ISBN 9780262542609 (paperback)
Subjects: LCSH: Sex role. | Sex. | Gender identity—Social aspects. | Sexual minorities—Identity.
Classification: LCC HQ1075 .S755 2021 | DDC 305.3—dc23
LC record available at https://lccn.loc.gov/2020040790

10   9   8   7   6   5   4   3   2   1

For
beloved members of
the School for Cultural and Social Transformation

and
enduring "kin" who read me:
Becky H.
Natalie A.
Adam W.
Lisa D.
and, always,
Shelley W.

CONTENTS

SERIES FOREWORD

The MIT Press Essential Knowledge series offers accessible, concise, beautifully produced pocket-size books on topics of current interest. Written by leading thinkers, the books in this series deliver expert overviews of subjects that range from the cultural and the historical to the scientific and the technical.

In today's era of instant information gratification, we have ready access to opinions, rationalizations, and superficial descriptions. Much harder to come by is the foundational knowledge that informs a principled understanding of the world. Essential Knowledge books fill that need. Synthesizing specialized subject matter for nonspecialists and engaging critical topics through fundamentals, each of these compact volumes offers readers a point of access to complex ideas.

Prepare to enter a story that is yours, however strange it could end up seeming.

Fascinating, fraught, intimate to everyone, gender increasingly has our attention as something newly morphing.

Is this newness new? Why does it seem so? The answers are surprising, involving numerous twists and turns. Given its intimacy to your own life, would you say you know—how would you say—what gender *is*? A common belief is that a person's "sex" is determined by genitals or something biological, whereas one's "gender" is cultural behavior, appearance, and mindset. Both, it is said, affect one's "sexual orientation."

This heated trio—sex, gender, sexuality—is far more startling than these terms suggest. Inspecting (our) gender tells us why. I aim to lure you into gender's import— its bewitching pleasures and falsifications, its concerning history, its enduring puzzles as a wily system—by meeting the moment of where we are. I can imagine a lucid, flat-footed version of this topic, but that doesn't interest me.

Taking a questioning approach to gender, I'll engage queries. Nodding to the interest in the genders now in play, I'll cut a path through the *when, why,* and *what* of the thing called "gender." Whether you're a parent, student, or kid—new to these matters or expert on them—gender is a realm you've been made to enter. If you move in the world as nonbinary, trans, or genderqueer, if you feel the force of racialized gender as a person of color, gender is something you have been questioning. Why not dive in now anew?

There is an arc to what I present. After we plunge into gender's strangeness—no matter how "normal" the concept seems—I will then turn to its unexpected history, involving trans and intersex kids, alongside feminists and female slaves, for this is the background of your own gender, whoever you may be. (There is also money running through this history. Money's in your gender in ways you may not think.)

This surprising background will help propel a question that grounds this book and foregrounds race: who is my opposite, my opposite sex? *If there are no opposites*, if there have always been multiple sexes in the United States (to be explained), then the sex duo—female/male—undergirding gender comes undone.

Which returns us to this moment. What's to be done with this undoing? How is gender tied to—all tied up with—capacities and debilities of bodies at this time? Why should we care? What urgencies remain?

The present is where I begin and end.

To ease your movement through this book, each of my chapters starts with a "short take." These are brief previews to tell you where you're going.

Here, in addition, are succinct chapter summaries:

Introduction: Is Gender a Piece of Cake?

No. If gender were simple, you wouldn't need this book. How to prepare for gender's tangled scene? How to prepare for surprises coming on the back of biology? With cake, to start, and then the likes of dolls, soldiers, and a certain Black gay rapper with a country flare—and more, of course. Here race and money are explained as two of gender's key ingredients.

1   Gender's Queer for Everyone?

Yes. Ask biology. Now we're prepared to query how biology—the baby's sex, the gender of children, the issue of hormones—is just so strange. How it is true that gender's queer for everyone hinges on the meaning of "queer" in this book, so we dive in. Racial oppression and racial exuberance build in this chapter. Money appears in our shoes and on a stage.

2 When Was Gender?

Do you know the history of this concept that has formed you? Twists and turns abound. As my preface states, intersex and transgender children, feminists, and enslaved Black women are central to your narrative—in arresting ways. In this mix are roots for Black Lives Matter, queer migration politics, and the field of gynecology.

3 Who's My Opposite?

It's been said so often, "opposites attract." Attraction has depended on opposite sexes—"men" and "women"— that are drawn together by the force of opposition. Race confounds this notion by multiplying sexes. Race makes a mess of the "hetero" and "homo" of sexual orientation. To see exactly how, we encounter restrooms, Black Panther writings, exclusions of Asians, and Native genderings.

4 Alluring Surface, Mysterious Depth

Genitals, skin, and clothes come together as gender's surface forms. Surface, however, runs so deep. It gets in our heads to form our very thoughts. Are we on our way to surface creativity—a riot of genders—that would not presume set traits, mindsets, and exclusions? Since race and money mix with gender, where is change headed? Disability and debility enter on this note and call for system change. One word gets the last word—fiercely so.

INTRODUCTION:
IS GENDER A PIECE OF CAKE?

Short take:
Gender(s) imagines that what we call *gender* has formed us all—from thrill to terror to points in between—right from our birth.

Did you know gender when you were born? Profoundly, you couldn't. Gender *becomes* something you know. But what do you know? What might remain deeply unknown about your own gender and all that surrounds it? I wonder how you (and all of us) grasp race and money in our gender. You could say this wondering shapes my every thought. Watch as I grow it from spark to burning issue—aflame and flowering always in gender.

Gender dramatically takes a path through you—personally, emotionally, politically, and conceptually. Now turn the tables. Take a path through *it*. How would you tell the story of gender? Where would you start? The story of gender is just so huge. Biology, I'm guessing, springs to mind for many. Wouldn't we need to start right there? Wouldn't biology easily ground us? Wait just a moment. Biology is coming in chapter 1, as you might suspect—there will be genitals, brain sex, hormones (!). But, most importantly, there will be surprises.

So, we begin by preparing for surprise.

Anyone who has dared to fight with gender (if you are transgender, nonbinary, or feminist) also might prepare, need to prepare, to consider how biology turns strange for everyone—*especially* for people who assume gender is given and "natural." (In my lifelong fight with gender, I was surprised to discover this fact. No one prepared me.)

This introduction is playful preparation.

Here we begin with a party phenomenon that has caught fire. It concerns birth, where babies don't choose their gendered fate. That would seem to settle it. You are what you're told you are. But that doesn't settle it. Now there's an upsurge in "choosing" your gender—maybe in childhood, maybe later—making gender a kind of buffet. *That's* too easy. We'll learn why. (Prepare for race and money.) Somewhere between settled fate and gender choice, the squirrely tale of gender awaits our contemplation.

Three key claims and a crisp mantra will offer lifelines for reading this book. (They are just ahead.) What follows is playful and dead-dog serious. We track change. Gender *has* changed? Our exhibits, with their quirks, are dolls, soldiers, electable female candidates, women's colleges, the term *Latinx*, and Lil Nas X, the country rapper.

After such a foray, *Gender(s)*' first chapter rewards you with "sex." But, first, there's cake.

Gender Is a Piece of Cake?

Some say it is.

The rise of the "gender-reveal party" literally makes gender cake. Someone slices a decorated baked good, maybe with a flourish, using a sword, and there it is: the baby's "gender" is revealed for all to see. The color pink or blue, fixed in a mixture of flour and sugar, says "girl" or "boy." All while the baby is baking still in utero.

And yet one wonders, with a dose of tenderness, if the cake-people protest a bit too much. Why such parties now? Why such an effort to show "what you are having" in having a baby? Why the word *gender* for what has conventionally been called a baby's *sex*? Could it be that gender needs new clarity in the form of color emerging from a cake?

Why no cake for race?

Plain old trendiness may explain these parties. They've caught fire. (More than five hundred thousand videos—and counting—have been put online, proving the popularity of "gender reveals.") But they've literally caught on fire. CNN, reporting on "reveals" gone wrong, tells of one party from 2017 in the state of Arizona: "Expectant father Dennis Dickey, an off-duty US Border Patrol agent, shot a target reading 'Boy,' which he had packed with the highly explosive substance Tannerite. The target emitted a blue cloud of smoke, but also ignited the surrounding brush. The flames spread to the Coronado National Forest, becoming the destructive Sawmill Fire" and burning around forty-seven thousand acres to the tune of $8 million in damage.[1]

As the saying goes, you can't make this up. Some wild metaphor concerning the dangers of our simplifying gender, making it something we just reveal, seems to lurk here (a border agent shooting a target, after all). Never mind the fact that the blogger who started the party phenomenon now regrets its spread, writing in July 2019: "Plot twist! The baby from the original gender reveal party is a girl who wears suits. She says 'she' and 'her' and all of that, but you know she really goes outside gender norms."[2]

Put the cakes aside. Is the scene of gender more like a buffet? Is there now a bounteous spread of genders—a spread of identities—from which to choose? Perhaps you've heard these phrases, or maybe not at all: "I'm a dandy butch." "I'm a farm feminist who is feminine." "I'm a straight fellow who likes to cook." "I'm a tiger mom who is bothered by this term." "I'm a Blacktina Native American, calling bullshit on white-people genders." "I'm a gay 'otter.'" "I'm a qtpoc (queer trans person of color)." "I'm agendered." There's your buffet? Indeed, these phrasings might well sound like an odd, consumerist, Amazon bonanza of gender-as-a-many-flavored thing. (Tinder added "37 new genders" in 2016.[3])

Look a little closer. Amid what sounds like playfulness, and a new inventiveness—I'm for both of these—one can sense a *reply* to the *systems* that have forged our gender. (Race threads in and out of these phrasings.)

Something profound registers here. Genders are words, as much as anything. (People slicing cakes are themselves eager to reveal one word—"boy" or "girl"— massive in its meanings.) It's a bit arresting to fully grasp this fact. The little cellular ant-like word mightily carries worlds on its back. Entire structures, societal systems, and institutions—those molding gender—come to us on the backs of words. These mighty system-bearing, structure- carrying words attach themselves to us (our bodies, our clothing, our gestures, our minds).

Not a piece of cake, then, not a buffet. Gender's something else. (Just start thinking about your own gender—what you think has formed it, how you would describe it, the manner of its attachment to your person.) Whatever it is, it's on the move. Gender is expanding in the US. It can feel explosive.

If you're a parent, you may feel baffled. Where did this come from all of a sudden? Confusion may be your reigning emotion. Perhaps you confess you struggle over pronouns, as if the word "they" for a singular person can't make sense—despite some straight guys stating a preference for "they" for themselves.[4] Or you may be gleeful, if you're genderqueer, to finally see the collapse of strict gendering, surprised even so that breakouts from gender are getting real traction. (Where was this expansion when I was a child?) Those of us teaching these matters for years, teaching that gender can't be truly binary, can't be a twoness, can't be free of money, can't shake race, can't avoid massive political entanglements, *can't stand apart from debilitating forces*, were considered "interesting," even "fascinating," back in the day—as if we were teaching science fiction. "That's cool to contemplate," students would remark. "It will never happen." It was always happening. . . .

Now it's apparent. People named "boys" or "girls" at birth may at times rename themselves newly, differently, creatively, strangely. And the standard terms—"woman," "man," "girl," "boy"—receive new contents wildly, unwittingly, also mundanely, changing the meaning of even these words. If a man wears a dress, does "man" change in meaning? (Billy Porter, star of *Pose*, seems game to find out. Wearing a "tuxedo gown" to the Oscars, then a "uterus dress" to the Tonys, he has been described as "the cause of the emasculation of the black man"—no small charge. Clearly amused, Porter replies: "I didn't know I had that much power . . . you can expect me to be wielding it every . . . chance I get."[5]) Gender is shifting—maybe it's melting—under our feet.

So if you're confused, curious, or adamant about these changes—or maybe you want to better explain them—this is your book. Enter this text and build a better argument. Argue with *me*. How did we get here? Why does it matter?

Gender can be a joyful expanse—and a tortured, torturing system. Gender has been central to forces of injustice and income inequality. And it touches everyone.

Just Remember This

If gender really were a piece of cake, how simple it would be to write its story. And how simple it would be to "give advice"—to anxious parents or eager gender-benders. "Just do this if you want to conquer gender. . . ."

Alas, for all its dramatic interest and life inside our flesh, gender is a serpentine matter to explain. Having three claims as lifelines to grasp (as a "just remember this") may help you follow the road (the ride?) ahead.

Might there be a mantra?

"Not cake, not buffet" doesn't quite cut it, if one seeks one small phrase to capture gender. "Word and system"— gender is forged at the scales of word and system—is a truer mantra, but not exactly sexy. Still, if you commit to memory "word and system," you will have a good bit of gender in a nutshell, as a place to start. Then, you'll be ready to open up the "system" part of this mantra, where race and money especially play their parts.

Also, you'll be primed for a weird effect of gender, captured by that phrase "word and system." Namely, how gender is forged both *above* and *below* the individual. That seems strange for something that lodges in our bodies, on our clothes, in our gestures, in our minds. But, if you think about it, that seems right. Gender seems delivered almost from on high, from a place outside us, more powerful than we are. (That's why the border agent shooting a target to reveal a baby's gender makes such a picture. Before the baby has even been born, its borders are established by the shooting of a word that explodes with force. "Boy!" That word is all of three letters.) Words are tiny things that run through our bodies in a steady stream. They are much smaller than individuals—yet we're "made" of words as much as made of cells.

"Word and system" as a mantra reminds us that we don't control our gender—surely not fully—and our parents don't either. Gender is streaming above us and below us. And though it's the aim of *Gender(s)* to reveal the juicy set of binds surrounding "sex" and "gender" as a pair of terms, it may be useful to rehearse some standard meanings—to see what they assume.

"Sex" has been the term, according to the *Merriam-Webster Dictionary*, for "either of the two major forms of individuals that occur in many species and that are distinguished respectively as female or male especially on the basis of their reproductive organs and structures." (Or, for a shortcut, adds my laptop's dictionary: "a person's genitals.") "Gender," by contrast, is "the behavioral, cultural, or psychological traits typically associated with one sex."[6] We can see how it's happened that "sex" connotes biology ("male" and "female") while "gender" designates cultural influence—dress, behavior, and invisible psyche ("masculine" and "feminine"). This can sound so clear. Sex is biological. Gender is cultural. Sex is gender's biological anchor.

It's helpful to state this boldly at the start. *Because this falls apart.* Sex and gender are *each* going to slide. Biological sex in chapter 1—including your genitals—is going to get unsteady in fascinating ways. And gender will be shown being pulled in directions that attempt to anchor it—even though its strangeness cannot be contained. Prepare for two banana peels. Sex is peel one; gender's peel two. (There will be laughter and debilitating falls.)

One more confusion. One persistent problem is the tendency we've seen for "gender" to be used where "sex" would have seemed the expected term. (Think of the "gender-reveal" celebrations' calling the baby's "sex" its "gender.") Does this show that gender has tended to remain largely binary in US conceptions? "Transgender," for some, could give this impression. "Trans" could mean only the movement from one fixed pole to another. (You could be "trans" and salute this binary. Or not at all.) Now, more commonly, "transgender" also names those who do not feel right in their sex assigned at birth, whether or not they seek a biomedical intervention.[7] If you sense the latter group could be massive, you're sensing how

Gender is queer.
By which I mean
irredeemably strange,
ungraspable, out of sync
with "male" and "female,"
weirdly not normal,
since lived gender fails
to conform to normative
ideals and expectations,
even when it is played
quite straight.

the borders among these central terms are spectacularly changing.

Now to the claims my book will explain. The pleasure (and terror) of these claims will be yours only after you encounter them in full. Here they are in brief:

Gender is queer. By which I mean irredeemably strange, ungraspable, out of sync with "male" and "female," weirdly not normal, since lived gender fails to conform to normative ideals and expectations, even when it is played quite straight. Conventional views try to snuff this strangeness, yet *conventional views are strange*.

Try this on for a very queer idea: raise two human beings to think they're opposites; give them opposite traits to embody; establish different mindsets, behaviors, and interests; offer them opposite aesthetics to pursue. Then ask these opposites to live together, love together, parent together as they raise little opposites; call this "marriage as it was intended"; call this "normal" gendering. Isn't this strange?

Gender is made of things that are not gender: race and money. Gender is fundamentally raced and classed in these United States (which is the central scene for this book). The history of the concept "gender" bears this out, in ways that may amaze you. When we know this history, the notion of "opposite sexes" falls apart.

In fact, the notion of there being "two sexes" forcefully crumbles.

I will claim we've never had two sexes in this country. Since the thirteen colonies, we have often made legal and biological distinctions between at least six categories (are they six sexes?): white man, white woman, Black man, Black woman, Native man, Native woman . . . joined by other sexes in other territories. There can be no opposites with six or more sexes. Due to the US system of race, the "opposite sex" is a phantom concept. Nobody lives it. Yet what stunning power it wields. It's had consequences (what an understatement) for this country's *dealings* with race.

Then there's money.

I say money because these dynamics are broader than class. (Only Americans, I'm tempted to say, would create classes—the underclass, lower middle class, middle class, upper middle class, or "working families"—that obscure class. US class is hard to name.[8]) Money, moreover, covers consumerism and much more. So, there's money . . .

. . . and there are words.

We put the words "girl" or "boy" *in* **kids.** This is an intrusion to which they don't consent and to which they must respond—their whole lives long. I know this thought is strange. It's just that I aim to remind us that words, to be words to us, must get inside us—must come in through a bodily orifice (ear or eye) or a finger reading Braille.

Sex and gender are *each* going to slide. Prepare for two banana peels. Sex is peel one; gender's peel two. (There will be laughter and debilitating falls.)

Words enter us and words live inside us, birthing whole realms of meaning *in* us. Words are even draped on us. We wear "girl" or "boy," for instance, in the form of clothes and hair and so much more. It can be hard, to put it mildly, to get words off of us—especially words put onto us before we were born. (I found so much to say about how we're made of words—how we make them out—I wrote a book about it.[9])

Now you have a mantra ("word and system"—sadly no sexier by force of repetition) with my three claims to lead you through this book. Let the games begin.

How is gender changing—or is it not?

Money and Race at the Gender Buffet: The Case of Dolls

The doll is quite the canary in the coal mine. It tracks change. Now it's implying a gender buffet. Some parents love what they're seeing surface in the land of dolls. Some parents sense a danger alert.

What has emerged? In the scene of kids and toys, dolls have marked a line between girls and boys. The dictate has been trumpeted: "boys don't play with dolls." Of course some do, but their boyness is questioned—almost seems wounded—the minute a doll is spotted in their hands, unless they're bashing it. Hence the use of the phrase "action figure" for G.I. Joe and dolls of his ilk. (It's like Grecian Formula and Just for Men coloring: hair dye for men that can't be "hair dye" since it's for men—a gem of gender's circular logic.)

Here comes a doll, then, to buck this history. *Time* magazine, which reports on this development, titles its article "A Doll for Everyone," exclaiming that "Mattel is on a mission to break taboos and shatter stereotypes . . . by introducing a gender-neutral doll."[10] One might reply that Mattel is on a mission to shatter its own bold stereotypes—still on offer through the toys it sells. But that would be getting ahead of ourselves. First, there's the doll. "In our world," states a Mattel advertisement, "dolls are as limitless as the kids who play with them. Introducing Creatable World.™"[11] (Stop right here and note the charming irony of the "TM" affixed to this naming. Mattel might as well be shouting "it's trademarked! it's ours! hands off! we own the label!") The ad continues with nary a pause: "a doll line designed to keep labels out and invite everyone in—giving kids the freedom to create their own customizable characters again and again."

Welcome to the gender buffet, it appears. It's not uncool. I would have wanted one—someone to keep my G.I. Joe company. (He seemed lonely.) But how does one make a doll to be so various, so apt to shape-shift? Clothes and hair and lissomness. *Time* describes the doll: "Each doll in the Creatable World series looks like a slender

7-year-old with short hair, but each comes with a wig of long, lustrous locks and a wardrobe befitting any fashion-conscious kid: hoodies, sneakers, graphic T-shirts in soothing greens and yellows, along with tutus and camo pants."[12] We're also told by *Time* that Mattel's first advertisement "featured a series of kids who go by various pronouns— him, her, them, xem," thus embracing trans and nonbinary kids. All so important. All so bending of the culture of dolls.

And race and money are deeply in this mix. To make this observation is not to downplay change. Or negate a change in play—the way kids play. (*They* queer toys.) The point is to grasp how gender has racialization running through it, in ways that remain taboo to engage. If you're wondering, then, what *Time* has to say about these dolls' racial aspects? It says nothing—as if gender-neutral were neutral on race, or just a topic to itself. The reader may be curious, however, about how race is "handled" on the doll's face—a color coat on an Anglicized visage?—when *Time* states: "Carefully manicured features betray no obvious gender: the lips are not too full, the eyelashes not too long or fluttery, the jaw not too wide." And the hair? *There* it is. The Black-skinned Creatable World™ doll is called "Deluxe Customizable Doll Kit Black Braided Hair" and comes with . . . no blonde hair. Race is not interchangeable here, and that may make all kinds of parents happy. *Time* doesn't speak of it. You can have race at the gender buffet as long as its "variety" is not interrogated. That would not be playful.

Mind you, *Time* explores the risk Mattel is taking with parents' reactions to this doll's gendering: "It's parents who are making the purchasing decisions, and no adult is going to have a neutral reaction to this doll." There were focus groups. Some parents, you would guess, were less than pleased. The doll "feels political," a parent complained. "Is it transgender?" another one asked. "How am I supposed to have a conversation with my kid about that? It's just too much. Can't we go back to 1970?" (Somewhere David Bowie is laughing.)

But even *Time* notes that Mattel knows what it's doing. "The company is betting" on where the country's going. Where it is going means money for Mattel. Forget focus groups; demographics tell the story. Gender nonconforming kids are on the rise, though it's hard to put a number on this "population" growth. In the words of *Time*: "Those kids are an untapped demographic. Mattel currently has 19% market share in the $8 billion doll industry; gaining just 1 more point could translate into $80 million in revenue for the company."

Play does not require store-bought toys. Kids are changing gender with quite surprising props. Really creatable worlds are here—and we need to mark them with nonconforming memoirs and other modes of listening. Here's the gender expanse that's exuberant. But we're not naive. Money's in our gender.

Race is, too. Only a century or so ago, white girl-children learned to bash dolls. As we glean from Robin Bernstein's *Racial Innocence: Performing American Childhood from Slavery to Civil Rights*, so much depends on dolls in pain. You heard that right. The thought of such a sensation for a doll, for a Black doll—the sense that it could recoil with hurt, if you were to hit it—tells us volumes about white girlhood from the time of slavery up to civil rights. (Or right now, in the George Floyd time of May 2020.)

Who feels suffering and so needs shielding from it? Who has sensitivity to possible harm? Children rehearse these relations with their dolls. Bernstein tells us the doll is a "prompt" for a set of actions connected to feelings.[13]

And at the height of the nineteenth century, new kinds of dolls were made for white girls. Dolls good for bashing—for proving that Blacks did not feel pain. As Bernstein documents, Black dolls were whipped, thrashed, and beaten, even directly according to the narrative of *Uncle Tom's Cabin*, and yet were seen to grin through it all. Their black color, their manufactured smiles, and their black rubber ("gutta-percha, a form of resilient rubber used in nineteenth-century dolls to enable them to survive rough play") helped script the "fun" recalled by former children.

The doll *is* a canary in the coal mine. And if the group One Million Moms, whose mission it is to "fight indecency," finds that Mattel's new doll in its neutrality "promote[s] a sinful lifestyle," "endanger[ing] our children," the group might read some history.[14] Just for doll perspective.

What Can the Figure of the Soldier Tell Us?

Soldiers and dolls assuredly make for an odd couple. Gender, nonetheless, joins them at the hip.

The soldier is a battleground. Just like dolls, the soldier sounds alarms that something is amiss, according to someone, in terms of gender change. The immediate matter involves servicepersons who identify as "trans." Indeed, once again, transgender Americans are banned from entering service. (As with all bans, democracy for everyone is affected.)

But there's a more hidden matter to unmask—one with consequences for everyone's gender. Remarkably, despite the soldier's vaunted manliness, perhaps no other figure, for several centuries, shows how contradictory the thing called "masculinity" truly is. If we need an entrée into gender's queerness—how it's strange for everyone—the soldier provides it.

First, however, we need to grasp why transgender Americans are being banned from service. The stated answer is actually money. Thus, while Mattel is busy breaking taboos in the name of trans and nonbinary (and all kinds of) kids—while it makes money in its bid to do right—money is the federal government's rationale for its discrimination on the basis of servicemembers' gender expression. Of course, the government denies there is a "ban" or any "discrimination" at all in what it's doing. Defense Department spokesperson Jessica R. Maxwell puts the matter this way: "If you are a transgender individual, you are welcome to serve"; the policy "actually prohibits discrimination on the basis of gender identity for accession, retention, or separation."[15]

What's the catch? What is the Trump policy excluding that the Obama administration was allowing (only starting in 2016)? To put it plainly, transgender prospects enlisting after April 2019 cannot receive gender-affirming health care and can only serve according to their sex assigned at birth. In more official language, the policy has ceased "presumptive accommodations" for people "diagnosed" with "gender dysphoria"—"a serious health condition," as Maxwell puts it. (A dictionary definition of "gender dysphoria" doesn't mention health and hints at how widespread it could be: "the condition of feeling one's emotional and psychological identity to be at variance with one's birth sex."[16]) Obama's policy still required that transgender servicemembers, to receive their health care, be "diagnosed" with "gender dysphoria"—no small thing. But the Trump policy seems to be saying the government will make no "accommodations" (a critical word for disability rights) for this apparent dysphoria-disability.

The knot of gender-change-meets-disability awaits us at the end of this book. Here just mark that government systems, with their monies, force a tradeoff. Want your health care? Confess a disability (Obama's policy). Or (Trump's policy): say whatever you want about your gender; your diagnosis will get you no health care, save you no money, and *we'll* sex you.

A series of presidential tweets says it all: "After consultation with my Generals and military experts, please be advised that the United States Government will not accept or allow . . . transgender individuals to serve in any capacity in the U.S. Military. Our military must be focused on decisive and overwhelming . . . victory and cannot be burdened with the tremendous medical costs and disruption that transgender in the military would entail. Thank you."[17] This was a twofer. "Medical costs" were one rationale for Trump's non-allowance (though these costs were tiny in the scheme of things). "Disruption" by "transgender in the military" was the other.

We've been down this road before. Who can forget all the "expert" testimony by the military brass about effects on troops' "morale" if gays weren't banned from military service? Back then, generals focused on the harm to soldiers and sailors and airmen if a guy knew an openly gay man served beside him—and just might desire him. The thought of attraction directed at them left men quaking in their boots, we were to gather. (By contrast, servicewomen's charges of rape were going ignored, even as an issue to be discussed.[18])

Money saves the day? Was it too discredited for Trump's administration—and, frankly, embarrassing to soldiers themselves—to play the fear card nakedly again? ("Disruption" is so wonderfully vague.) Is the money matter the best beard available for this new installment of bold discrimination? As of this writing, the trans ban stands.

So does something else: the striking revelation of gender nonconformity at the soldier's core. The argument I am about to make could occur to you (as it did to me) while reading Michel Foucault's famous treatise *Discipline and Punish: The Birth of the Prison*.[19] But, really, it's so obvious that readers might take it as a gender truism. Here's the heart of it. The soldier is the most obedient, subservient, subjugated, dominated, movable, *docile* body there is. The soldier is literally made to obey.

If we encountered this description somewhere else, we might well think it referred to the stereotype of conventional femininity, so opposite does it seem to conventional masculinity. That's not all. Equally striking is the fact that, like a pin-up or a kind of mannequin, the soldier is interchangeable with others of his type. "Individuality"—a signpost of manliness—is clearly vanquished. The soldier, like the worker, becomes a kind of cog. Foucault even offers an abstract phrase that becomes chillingly literal in war: the soldier is a "fragment of mobile space," he says, to be moved at will in whatever direction the Command determines.

Viewing documentaries such as the acclaimed *World War I in Color* proves these claims and prepares us for grasping new binds for boys (in the next chapter).[20] Throughout the documentary, the soldier's masculinity slips on and off—becoming indistinguishable from feminine traits. For example: the "swishing of kilts" on parade—the glamor of soldiers' military uniforms—becomes a soldier's seduction into soldiering;[21] there is quaking fear ("if anyone tells you he wasn't afraid, he's a damned liar"); some men's disfigurements (turning blue from poison gas) echo those of women (who turn yellow from making TNT); men ask wives "to keep a brave heart for me."

Gone is the posture and dignified bearing of the soldier as a blazon. What is revealed is a docile body—albeit a violent docile body. From a "symbol of national pride" to a "posture of total dejection," says the narrator, "chivalry here took a final farewell." At the Battle of the Somme, the Allied troops advanced "just seven miles with 600,000 casualties." That meant eighty-six thousand men—like cogs being moved—were required to die for each mile gained.

The soldier was a fragment of mobile space.

Taking Stock of Gender Change

Change, by definition, is a liquid force, not so easy to capture in the moment. Historical backdrops help gauge change. Taking stock requires that we jet back in time, and then return to the blazing "now." And such stocktaking asks us to learn how the past still rumbles inside our gender(s).

"The Electable Female Candidate," a satire published in the *New Yorker* in 2019, reminds us of just how much hasn't changed for women in politics, despite their growing numbers. The piece is hilarious because it rings so true:

> The electable female candidate reaches across the aisle with soft moisturized hands. She knows how to fire a gun, but also has never held a gun, and doesn't know what a gun is. She's becoming a vegan, but stands behind Arby's in its commitment to the Meats. . . . She's able to radically reshape society, but moderately. She was raised on a farm in the middle of Central Park. . . . She went to Harvard, but hated it. . . . She is Beyoncé. . . . She wears sensible shoes that are hot. . . . She loves babies, even the ugly ones, although she has never participated in a gender-reveal party.[22]

The joke is that women, unlike their counterparts, have to be "all things to all people" if they would succeed. Evidently, they have to be just like men *and* women, in their womanly way of being.

Woman = man + woman? We laugh because it's weird—and so recognizable. Even as conditions on the ground change for women, as they increasingly enter historically masculine roles, they must do men's work while they preserve a woman's way of doing it, which *includes* manliness. Women are (asked to be) two sexes. Yet there's also race. Women, in being all things to all people according to this satire, must be *not too white*— Beyoncé is the satirical measure—and not *too* elite—in order to appeal. All these words wobble, yet the point remains. Gender as we've known it also swallows change. The binary of sex *and* gender is just dazzlingly durable, as change reigns.

And that's the fix we're in. So much about the sex/gender system stays in place while dramatic changes seem to swirl around us. Both change and stasis are happening together, *at the same time*. No surprise, then: "gender reveals" are burgeoning just when "gender-creative" parenting of "gender-free" children is on the rise. Still, no matter how creative this spawning of children proves to be, systems of gender—and the words for gender—lie in wait for children. Even if their infanthood is washed of definitive signs attached to *them*, they are still caught in the torrents of gender that surround them (the gendering of their parents, teachers, neighbors, and celebrities),

The joke is that women, unlike their counterparts, have to be "all things to all people."

Woman = man + woman? We laugh because it's weird—and so recognizable.

making these newfangled children like salmon swimming upstream, despite the delight of this different swim.

So, what is happening in terms of gender change? One big case is telling: the bind for women's colleges surrounding . . . "woman." It could sound puzzling—or completely cheering—but they don't know what a woman is. Shockingly, or not, historic women's colleges are having a crisis over the *word* that defines their institutions. It is philosophical while it's just so practical. Who can be admitted? This has gotten hard—for definers and defined.

Here's what tripped this wire. Historic women's colleges had to take a stand as transgender students sought admission. (The colleges in question are "the seven sisters": the colleges founded *because* the Ivy League did not admit undergraduate "women" until the 1970s. Harvard, evidently, knew a woman when it saw one.) Of these "sister" schools, Mount Holyoke College, in 2014, crafted the most expansive policy, listing seven categories that can be admitted:

Biologically born female; identifies as a woman

Biologically born female; identifies as a man

Biologically born female; identifies as other/they/ze

Biologically born female; does not identify as either woman or man

Biologically born male; identifies as woman

Biologically born male; identifies as other/they/ze and when "other/they" identity includes woman

Biologically born with both male and female anatomy (Intersex); identifies as a woman

Those who are born biologically male and identify as male cannot apply.[23]

We will return to the all-important phrase "biologically born": much has hung on this hook throughout the years. For now, we should notice that what is called "sex"—male or female—does not rule the day for this policy change from 2014 for the oldest women's college in the US. "Identifying" does. If you hook yourself to the *word* "woman," in some measure—or unhook from it in approved ways— you can come in. Word and system will admit you.

Wellesley, by contrast, draws a tighter circle. They do not include trans men in their policy or this category offered by Mount Holyoke: "biologically born male, but identifies as other/they or ze and when 'other/they' identity includes woman." For admission to Wellesley, one must "liv[e] as a woman and consistently identif[y] as a woman."[24] The trick is "consistently." (The *New Yorker* satire comes to mind.) Given that jobs and so many aspects of life require "masculine" traits, can women *live* their consistency "consistently"? I suspect Wellesley means to admit whoever walks under the *sign* woman.

Clearly, this crisis is over a word. (Word and system.) Other gender crises are over a letter.

"Latinx" has surfaced to hasten gender change. This new term, with its striking *X*, now appears in *Merriam-Webster Dictionary* as of 2018. Per Google, it's defined as "a person of Latin American origin or descent (used as a gender-neutral or nonbinary alternative to Latino or Latina)."[25] This change ignited in just a few years.

The force is with the *X*. It is the element—this one letter—that asks for *system* change, not just inclusion. Prior to the use of *X*, the term *Latino/a* (hard to pronounce and written as "Latin@" by many people) had arisen to include both men and women in a single word. "Latinx," however, was a move beyond this twoness and the binary of sex. Claudia Milian, in her book *LatinX*, takes us on a tour of these charged developments and captures their thrust when she cites activist Alba Onofrio: "We have a critique of the system, and we want to be entirely different and not just let in."[26] (Shades of the pressures put on women's colleges. Here, nonetheless, we don't have seven categories introduced by policy. We have a letter talked about in chat rooms.)

"X" is a portal to the unknown. An open horizon. In the face of gender's binary tendencies, "the 'X' turns away from the dichotomous toward a void, an unknown, a wrestling," say scholars Macarena Gómez-Barris and Licia Fiol-Matta. Indeed, there's a fascinating origin to the mathematical *X*, as we learn in the TED Talk by Terry Moore entitled "Why Is 'X' the Unknown?"[27] According to Moore, Spanish scholars from the medieval period were stumped by how to translate Arabic sounds like the letter "sheen." "Because you can't say 'sh' in Spanish," Moore informs us, *X* has played its role as the mathematical unknown.

Powerfully, as if she were spinning off this story, literary critic Gloria Elizabeth Chacón, as Milian shares with us, probes the *X* in the context of language and Indigenous Mesoamerican peoples. The *X* "is a confrontation," writes Chacón, "between the Latin and indigenous languages—a 'mother tongue' that refuses gendered language." "Feminine/masculine articles don't exist in Maya or Zapotec," but, she adds, "this does not mean that gendered ideologies are nonexistent"—"only that the X is the ineffable indigenous language that keeps returning." And, she says, "LatinX is an opening," "an ethical position that engages with indigenous populations."

"X," we could say, is where oppression and potentiality cross. "X," one can't forget, as Milian reminds us, also "stands for . . . indigenous groups 'sign[ing] over' their property . . . to colonizing Europeans," echoed in Malcolm X's affixing this symbol to his name. Portal and erasure meet in the *X*. No wonder Milian states her frustration, giving a feel for the not-yet-full embrace of Latinx:

"The X is unconventional. The X is multiplying. The X is complicated. The X is funky. I like the X. I don't like the X. . . . Will you pass it up or pass it on?" That's a clever question for the scene of gender change.

Genre, as it happens, is also in our gender. No one of late has more cunningly made genre into gender than Lil Nas X—himself an X-er (for no stated reason). What a genre breakout and sign of gender change has issued from his person, this fresh talent on the musical scene with his song and video "Old Town Road." When you thought you'd seen it all, a man on a horse rides into town—an old Western trope—but the town is LA and the man is Black. Even more important, the sound is a mix of country crawl and deep-base rap.

Here is keen exuberance.

Nothing feels heavy, only arresting in sheer surprise. The viewer's own startle is mirrored by the look of shock on the faces of neighborhood Black folks stopping in their tracks as they water the lawn, fix their cars, and gaze with amazement from the front porch. The figure before them is so unforeseen—a cowboy on their streets—a Black man in the genre of the cowboy outlaw (with that horse!)— they have to laugh, or dance in response.

And something about the gender on display—a boyish surface that is so playful, undefended, ironic, boldly declared, and just so able to morph into joyful, fringe-swinging glee—looks so new, maybe so gay, and is flat-out unexpected. It's about as likely as "Old Town Road" becoming "the longest-running No. 1 song" in US history—which it did.[28] And now that the singer, Lil Nas X, has come out queer—while his song topped the charts—people are reading all kinds of meanings into his lyrics, his gestures, his genres. His genre—what *is* it?—has become his gender, whatever *it* is.

Indeed, in the luckiest turn of all, "Old Town Road," while climbing the charts, ended up banned. For its genre-bending. It was said not to have "enough" country elements. There was pandemonium. Along came Billy Ray Cyrus for a remix—and the song went viral, straight to the top of the *Billboard* Hot 100. Not incidentally, the song in its witty weirdness has been praised for its embrace of "opposites." Not masculine/feminine (though the song runs the gamut on the gender spectrum). Not Black/white (though it ends with Nas and an old white woman, together in their get-ups, mugging for the camera). Not gay/straight (despite a queering of the cowboy). And not oppressive/liberating (even though the remix plays on themes of escape from a posse—Nas is holding a big bag of money—and lynching, if he's caught?).

Nas is wedding a different set of opposites: "two quintessential American musical genres": country and hip-hop (with, of course, their racial histories in attendance). Lil Nas X, says *Time* magazine, even stands for "democratized pathways to success," since Nas made his history-making hit with "a beat he purchased online for $30. . . . All this has the people who usually make money off stars like Lil Nas X questioning long-held assumptions about who consumes what, how, and when."

That's a bit utopian, especially when *Time* is eager to conclude that "Lil Nas X represents a more unified vision of the future, one in which a young queer black man can dominate popular culture." True, if the Grammys are the metric for this future, Nas is it. He was a vision as he staged his hit at the 2020 Grammy Awards. Springing from a couch in a silver cowboy suit, showing off an impossible sheen, Nas went strutting and skipping into other "boxes" of "boys" on a carousel-stage (among them, the Korean sensation BTS, itself a variously gendered "boy band," and young Mason Ramsey, the budding country star)—all before emerging in a long, black, Western, patent-leather cloak.

Boys are on the move. But the Grammys are not representative of life for Black queer men. Nas himself tweeted, with a humorous punch line: "Last year i was sleeping on my sisters floor, had no money, struggling to get plays on my music, suffering from daily headaches, now I'm gay."[29] These claims bear out my themes. Gender change is all around us. We measure it against the binaries that are alive and well—but themselves quite weird. Race and money flood our gender.

"Can't nobody tell me nothin'/You can't tell me nothin'," sings Lil Nas. These double negatives sound like an *X*—which, however jubilant, is not a piece of cake.

GENDER'S QUEER FOR EVERYONE?

Short take:
"Isn't a person's sex biological?"

Whoever you are, you may have asked this question. Maybe you're someone genuinely thinking the answer will settle matters neatly. If you're genderqueer, trans, or non-binary, among many others jousting with gender, you get asked this frequently. (Which doesn't mean you haven't pondered it yourself—to craft your best reply.)

Gender may be showing a raft of funkiness, but surely a reliable sex lies underneath our gender(s)? Gender expression cannot deny biology, it is often said, since we do have bodies—and they are biological. This familiar view still reigns in US medicine, psychology, and popular on-the-street belief.

But sex-as-gender's-anchor gets much stranger on examination. We will examine "sex assigned at birth"—

especially the claim that sex precedes gender and largely drives gender. Alongside this question of sex sits the question of sex hormones. Testosterone proves to be a wild story, revealing many oddities begging our attention, so we will attend.

Next, we'll delve into normative gender to see if and how it might be strange, despite its longstanding status as normal, even straight. Such an aim will take us into new, eye-opening interviews with "boys"—everyday boys, as they're presented—to hear their views on masculinity, sexuality, and relations with "girls." Following that scene, we'll enter into fantasies forged and held by "women," found in a striking, telling source. (Shoes are going to star.)

Then, we'll crescendo with takes on gender (they might be your own) not pretending normalcy—showing intertwinings of oppression and exuberance. These takes feature Black gay men "up in pumps" on "the floor" (the ballroom floor); Latinas' realm of gestures; brown boys and "rice queens."

Apparent is a world of enticing contradictions, showing why gender might be queer for everyone.

Queer, You Say?

Queer, you might be guessing, is not what one would think. Not everyone's gender is gay, to say the least. Lil Nas X may be considered a glimpse of the future—more creative genders to come—but his being gay does not extend to everyone.

What does "queer" mean?

Odd as it may seem, here it doesn't signify "LGBT," though this common rendering is of course included. I mean *queer* in its broadest sense. I mean *queer* as "strange." (Dictionaries offer this meaning for *queer*.) Or as previewed in the last chapter, *queer* here means: irredeemably strange, ungraspable, out of sync with "male" and "female," weirdly not normal, since lived gender fails to conform to normative ideals and expectations, even when it is played quite straight.

Gender's queer for everyone? Strikingly, it is. But the ways in which its oddities rule our lives—creating stunning privileges, letdown promises, daily navigations, or grueling debilities—highly differ. Still, there's a queerness running through gender and that is news to many.

It is time to sound this claim. Here are three scenarios of normative strangeness as an opening volley:

Consider, for Example:
One man, one woman. For the sake of argument, let's say I've seen their genitals, so I can vouch that their genitals are different. (These are friends, so I haven't seen their genitals; I'm going on faith.) He's a white professor; she is, too. Both went to Harvard—that's where they met—and

both did doctorates in the humanities. Both wear clothes from the GAP or J.Crew (or, when dressing up, they splurge on tweeds). Both are ambitious, professionally accomplished, occasionally witty, and relatively in touch with their emotions (for academics). Both report enjoying erotic stimulation of the same orifice (use your imagination).

Question: is this couple—so much the same in interests, racial designation, job, salary, dress, and even focus on bodily orifice—of the same gender but not the same sex? Are they homosexual in some strange sense?

Consider Next:
Same-sex marriage, same-sex sex: both now allowed by US law after centuries of non-allowance or criminalization. Here's a revealing historical problem, largely denied because it's too revealing: not all sameness is created equal; sameness itself is never the same.

Same-*class* marriage? Same-class sex? We're all about it. Ask Jane Austen. In her famous novels, so key is it to keep class consolidated and forms of property all in the family that no good heroine marries a "lover." (That would be too directly erotic.) No, she gains a lover by seeking a new outside "brother" for her sister and, most importantly, by marrying his house.

And same-*race* marriage? Same-race sex? So much do we love it, we tried requiring it in the US. As you may know, until 1967, you couldn't have hetero-race-sexuality in many US states. There were supposed to be white-on-white genitals, Black-on-Black genitals, though these samenesses were unequal. Is gender in this picture—or just sex (in terms of genitals)?

Here, once again, are race and money—now defining sexual orientation.

Consider Last:
What I've said to gynecologists: Imagine a woman coming to see you. She is suffering badly . . . from a word.

A word is literally making her sick (one she's worn like a skin-tight dress, a smothering surface she cannot remove). The patient is suffering from the word *woman*, the word attached to her surface from birth—a word that has formed her from the outside in, affecting how she sits, what tone she talks in, how she projects herself in space, what money she makes, and what she internalizes minute by minute, affecting her health.

This is a word that fails to distinguish between "sex" and "gender" at nearly every turn. In fact, most of us, *including gynecologists*, have never seen "sex." That's because sex is a layered thing (as we're going to learn). That's not all. Even if we did think genitals were sex, never in our lives have we seen them on their own. We only see the genitals of "girls" or "boys"—"women" or "men"—because there is gender glazing our eyes. Gender shapes the sex we think precedes it (as we will explore). That's how strange sex/ gender proves to be.

Sex, gender, sexuality. The labyrinth of gender turns on the pathways to and from these terms. Let's begin with sex—the kind we (believe we) see at birth.

Is There Sex Beneath Your Gender?

"Penis envy," that old chestnut offered by Freud, has long struck so many people as evidence of Freud's own obsession with the male organ as the be-all-and-end-all. To imagine that everything concentrates on genitals—the penis, most of all—just seems juvenile.

Yet in a way so familiar to us all, what awaits a newborn in the US proves a lasting obsession with . . . the penis. You have one or you don't. We see it or we don't. The visibility of this organ is the chief driver of sex assigned at birth. We put our eyes on the surface of the baby—and give it a read. If all looks as expected, we assign a word that "is" the baby's sex.

Just to repeat so we don't miss the point. Before there is sex, there is reading—and a word. A life-defining word awaits each baby. The word goes on paper and is spoken in the air, but there's no way to affix it to the body (short of tattooing it). The body is physically separate from its word. But the word will hover or function like a cone pulled down on the body. All without the baby's consent. Only later will the word *get inside* the child to become a word that stands for the child itself (if the child will stand for it).

Even more dramatically, the child's sex-word, pronounced at birth, is a gender-word: "it's a girl!" or "it's a boy!" The idiom is not "it's a male!" or "it's a female!" (Ah, those gender-reveal parties have stumbled onto something . . .) An entire world of *cultural* assumptions is rolled up into the word rolled onto the baby and its genitals. A reading of race is also taking place at the baby's birth—and it may appear on the baby's birth certificate—but it is not conventionally marked as the word for what the baby "is."

There's no cake for race. Far less commonly do people ask out loud (though they may be thinking it): "What are you having, a white or black baby?"[1] Nor do people ask, "Are you expecting a middle-class child?" And no one asks for the newborn's sexual orientation, since, historically, that has been *assumed*: the child will be straight unless attraction takes a turn (something "goes wrong") at a later point in time. More recently, some parents wait to learn what the grown child says about itself when it is sexual— "hopefully," many parents think, when the child is grown past childhood. (Fear of child sexuality reigns.[2])

But to go back to the baby's sex, there is more to say. There are fetal *layers* to the baby's sex, to put the matter oddly.

A life-defining word
awaits each baby. The
word will hover or
function like a cone
pulled down on
the body. All without
the baby's consent.

Anne Fausto-Sterling, the renowned biology and sex/gender expert, succinctly states: "By birth, the baby has five layers of sex."[3] Even more strikingly, "these layers do not always agree with each other." Here's the beginning, one is tempted to say, of our not agreeing with ourselves *biologically*. Parts of our body disagree with other parts. Baby sex-layers, moreover, is a concept Fausto-Sterling takes from famous researcher John Money—and Money, we will see, plays a critical role in what eventually gets called "gender." (Yes, a stunning pun emerges from his name. What has made gender is indeed Money.) Money also theorizes sex.

The naming of sex isn't luscious, but it's crucial. You should know your layers (what they're said to be):

Layer one is called "*chromosomal sex*-layer 1," comprised, no surprise, of the combination of X and Y chromosomes fetuses receive when an egg and sperm join. Layer two is "*fetal gonadal sex*" (testes or ovaries or, in some cases, a combination), followed by a third layer: "*fetal hormonal sex*" (resulting from hormones released by the gonads). This fetal hormonal sex "contributes to the formation" of layer four, named the "*internal reproductive sex*"—the one we *don't see*—and one that isn't "one," since for (the people called) males it's the grouping of vas deferens, prostate, and epididymis and for (the people called) females it's the collection of uterus, cervix, and Fallopian tubes. (Whether your "man or woman on the street" could name all these parts of their internal sex is an interesting question.) Lastly, generally around the fetus's fourth month of development, the fifth layer forms as "the hormones complete their job" in shaping the fetus's external genitalia: penis, scrotum, vagina, clitoris, and any number of variabilities and "genital ambiguities."

To state the obvious, adults who name the baby with a word, "girl" or "boy," see *only one* of the five sex-layers.

The others are invisible to the naked eye. Who knows how many discrepancies between and among the layers of sex go undetected. (You might be discrepant with yourself and not know it.) In the past, should a "problem"— disagreement (!)—arise, steps might well be taken to force the baby to agree with itself. The history of intersex people, with all its profound implications, sits right here.[4] And given the incidence of intersex, which might be as high as one in sixty people, it's a bigger history and bigger population than is often recognized. Also, a bigger struggle to be accorded human rights, instead of deemed a problem.

The overriding historical measure of this "problem" has been the viability of a baby's penis. Until recently, if a child would "suffer" an insufficient penis, something would be done: genital surgery, some form of treatment, and/or switching the word for the sex. A "boy" with a "bad" penis might be named and raised a "girl." (Who has penis envy in this scenario? The doctors, the parents, the projected future child—our culture at large?)

All of which takes us to a sixth layer. What is named "gender." It's as if binary sex (itself a five-layered process) passes its credentials to binary gender—thus the presumption that gender is a twosome, named as *either* "girl" or "boy." In the words of Fausto-Sterling: "this identification" of the child's sex from the child's "external genital anatomy" then "initiate[s] a social response that be[gins] the *gender* socialization of the newborn."[5] Except the gender system *has* been surrounding the newborn baby since before its birth. That's why the name of the "gender-reveal party" is, yes, so revealing. They are *indeed* revealing gender, as they say.

Welcome to the gender fort.

The "social response" to a baby is "intense." So intense, we learn, that our reading of its genitals, to which we pin a word, causes our building of a fort around this reading. It's no joke. Fausto-Sterling calls this socialization "gender fortification." The word "boy" or "girl," however cone-like, however body-sheath-like, is evidently not enough for us. We act as if we have to fortify it at every turn. So here come clothing, colors, toys, and hair.

While the child is building a basic body image, learning that its body has some kind of borders in space and time, and sensing through its senses, we are fortifying what it can't see or feel: a gender we're invested in, built around a sex the baby doesn't know. Bookmark this matter of not-knowing. Here a chasm opens. Call it the unconscious.

It's a place where the "enigmatic remnants" of, say, a parent's speech on a baby's skin—before the baby has become a speaking child—are held in mystery. "They persist as question marks without answers," says analyst Avgi Saketopolou.[6] What a rich realm of "disagreements" might be here—might brew here. "We" and "the baby" are treading different paths.

The baby is exploring, we are defining. Our defining just may affect its exploring. Unless there is "brain sex."[7] This contested concept holds that binary gender naturally follows in the footsteps of binary sex because *our brains are sexed*. (This is no small fortification of binary-ness. Later we will see other elements that ride to the rescue, as it were, of the binary sex/gender system so as to fortify the fort itself. Brain sex is a big one.) Fausto-Sterling goes so far as to call this (old) idea a meme. It emerged in the 1950s, after all, from a "germinal paper" and remains, she says, "a favorite hypothesis despite a lack of direct evidence" for its claims.

Brain sex means that boys and girls have different brains. To put it more precisely, brain sex is the claim that "fetal hormonal sex produces or causes brain sex differentiation." Or, again, it's the thought that fetal hormones, while the fetus was developing, "'organized' brain development in ways that might affect a wide variety of sex-differentiated behaviors"—and different mental abilities—because the fetus was "exposed to different

While the child is building a basic body image, we are fortifying what it can't see or feel: a gender we're invested in, built around a sex the baby doesn't know.

hormonal cocktails *in utero*." This might take the cake on there being two sexes that produce two genders.

But even brain sex believers raise problems for there being simple answers. Catherine Woolley, a neurobiologist at Northwestern University, says of this research: "One of the very big takeaways is that sex differences in the brain are real, but they're not about differences in cognition or behavior."[8] "You cannot extrapolate differences," she continues, "that appear on a molecular or structural level to differences in behavior." Scholar Gina Rippon, a self-described sex-difference denier, says: "We have to pay more attention to how our experiences drive our brain architecture."[9]

What drives what? Two quick points. One involves brain size; the other, brain connections. When Woolley and others point to brain differences, they often mean features like the size and weight of brains. Is the "boy" brain bigger? Researchers state over and over that there is great overlap in size for "men's and women's brains"— around a seventy percent overlap—"with small average differences between two groups."[10] There is no definitive evidence that size affects function, never mind behavior or cognition. Only conjecture takes you to that view.

Experiences, by contrast, make for connections— neural connections—that *change brains*. (Hence, Rippon's plea that "we have to pay more attention to how our experiences drive our brain architecture.") Fausto-Sterling reminds us that the newborn baby's nerve cells require "a lot of refinement" after birth. Relative to those of a five-year-old child, the newborn's nerve cells are "poorly connected." For the first five years of life, the human brain grows three to four times bigger, "mostly because those cells already present at birth become more and more complex and interconnected." By the time it is about three months old, the density of the child's synapses has doubled; by adulthood, the brain's branching of connections is almost eight hundred times what it is for the newborn baby.

That's a lot of change across the motor, behavioral, and cognitive fields of a person's life. And culture—gender's specialty—lies in that voluminous branching of connections. Gender, by this logic, changes human brains more than brain sex ever could, a fact that may explain how so many people disagree with their *brains*.

Brain sex, nonetheless, rises up again as another matter lands in our laps: the hormonal cocktail to which the fetus is "exposed" in utero. What's the deal with hormones?

Testosterone Is the Big Story

I do mean story.

"It has a slightly golden hue, suspended in an oily substance and injected in a needle about half as thick as a telephone wire."[11] This descriptive hook gives way to a first-person statement of wonder. A weird wonder. "I am so used to it now that the novelty has worn off. But every now and again the weirdness returns. The chemical I am putting in myself is synthetic testosterone: a substance that has become such a metaphor for manhood that it is almost possible to forget that it has a physical reality. Twenty years ago, as it surged through my pubescent body, it . . . made me a man. So what, I wonder, is it doing to me now?"

So begins a famous essay, "The He Hormone," published in 2000 by well-known journalist Andrew Sullivan. Sullivan considers his own experience with hormone-replacement therapy as biological evidence for the social differences and inequalities between men and women.

And so arrive the stories—and the scholarly analysis of these stories—about a hormone that gets to be known as a letter. Mighty "T."

In just this much of Sullivan's essay, there are things to note. Wondrously, Sullivan knows he's weirdly injecting a metaphor as much as anything—what he later calls "a syringe full of manhood." The question is: does his essay head toward "the physical reality" of testosterone (which for many scholars is messy, complicated, nuanced, and dynamic) or does he plunge headlong into myth? You can read his essay and see what you think. Subtlety is not what is likely to strike you.

Of his own experience, Sullivan writes: "Depression, once a regular feature of my life, is now a distant memory. I feel better able to recover from life's curveballs, more persistent, more alive." "My wit is quicker, my mind faster, but my judgment is more impulsive." "You are not helpless in front of it, but you are certainly not fully in control." "Then there's anger." And there are testimonials that Sullivan cites: "It makes me think more clearly," says one man. Another reports: "I walk into a business meeting now and I just exude self-confidence. I know there are lots of other reasons for this, but my company has just exploded since my treatment. . . . I feel capable of almost anything." And yet another: "It turned my life around. I felt . . . almost spiritually strong." Concludes Sullivan right at the start: "The power of that biology" "helps explain, perhaps better than any other single factor, why inequalities between men and women remain so frustratingly resilient in public and private life."

Sullivan's essay has been criticized in a piece called "The Lie Hormone" and put into question by scholarly books such as *Testosterone: An Unauthorized Biography*. So, there's much to argue.

What it prompts for *Gender(s)* is a set of layers of my own making, reminiscent of the baby's five sex-layers. Think of these as the gendered-body-layers of the taking of T. Here are six layers to consider if you end up injecting testosterone, whoever you are, however you're gendered, at whatever age:

1. Your chemical makeup heretofore

2. Your gender fort (how forces, including race and money, have gendered you)

3. Your beliefs about testosterone (influenced by your gender fort?)

4. Your taking of T (time of day, dosage, frequency, kind of T)

5. Your sensations

6. Your self-report

You might well notice that several of these layers would be difficult, if not completely impossible, for you to assess. Can you account for your chemical makeup writ large? Could you ever render the gender fortifications made upon your person, many of which happened when you were not yet conscious? How have your conscious beliefs about T given you a possible placebo effect (never mind your unconscious beliefs that you couldn't fathom if you tried)?

Such a layered lineup explains how we get such varied reports—such fervent testimonies. Likewise, it indicates how the "The He Hormone," strenuously countered by "The Lie Hormone," is supplemented by the highly informative study of the studies *and* stories on T in *Testosterone*. Sullivan, you would realize if you used my layers as a guide to reading him, largely stays inside layers five and six—though five is skimpy, despite his descriptions, and six is offered as authoritative data for what he has selectively read and believes.

He does hedge his bets by tipping his hat to layers two and three, but every concession turns toward a "but." "To be sure," he concedes, "because human beings are also deeply socialized, the impact of this difference is refracted through the prism of our own history and culture. But . . ." And, "No doubt my previous awareness of the mythology of testosterone had subtly primed me for these feelings. . . . But . . ."

A few key moments from Sullivan's essay show the problems surrounding all his "T talk."[12] Take his early slide into research on brain sex. Backing up the truck, he refers to fetal sex in a general sense: "You need testosterone to turn a fetus with a Y chromosome into a real boy, to masculinize his brain and body."[13] Before you know it, the evidence that a "real boy" is made in the womb is proven by (you guessed it) nonhuman rats. Sullivan explains: "Since it is unethical to experiment with human embryos by altering hormonal balances, much of the evidence for this idea is based on research conducted on animals."

What do rats do that must convince us of T's special powers? The female injected-with-testosterone rats develop "penises" from their "clitorises" and try having "sex with other females with merry abandon." Just ask a trans man (trans men, ask yourselves) if this experience always tracks with trans men who are female-assigned at birth and taking T as part of their transitioning: have they developed penises and do they always, naturally, mount females?[14] Many trans men prefer sex with men. Most do not attempt surgical phalloplasty since a working penis is still hard to make (and it takes money).[15] And what should we glean from Sullivan's sense of human behavior that he thinks having your testosterone blocked (as was done with male rats) of course makes "you"—human or rat—present yourself sexually "in a passive, receptive way"? Is this what women of any sort *biologically* do in the year 2020?

Doesn't the history of race in our country question inequalities attributed to T? Sullivan's early conclusion that hormonal differences "explain, perhaps better than any other single factor, why inequalities between men and women remain so frustratingly resilient" begs the question: is he thinking solely of white people? The *way* inequalities run inside African American communities, for example, do not fit the patterns Sullivan is imagining: "men" in Black communities, despite the "power" of their testosterone, have not naturally or historically exceeded Black "women" in opportunities, employment, advancement, or self-confidence.[16] The *Moynihan Report* on "the Negro Family" from 1965—a prejudicial study of major magnitude—made this point when it lamented Black men's feminized conditions in the face of Black folks' female-headed homes.[17]

Does Sullivan think that solving racism would free Black people into the more natural inequalities white people "frustratingly" find so resilient?

There are two tells to Sullivan's inability to grapple with race (and also money). Here's the first. When he himself admits that testosterone "is highly susceptible to environment"—it rises or falls in relation to circumstances—he gives an example of what he means. "Working women," he asserts, "have higher levels of testosterone than women who stay at home." Is he only thinking about professional women? Do immigrant maids, working in hotels or other people's houses, have elevated T? Has anyone checked?

One thing's for sure. When he does address race, he says some jolting things. Citing a study strongly critiqued in the book *Testosterone*, Sullivan states in his second tell: "Inner-city youths, often exposed to danger in high-crime neighborhoods, may generate higher testosterone levels than unthreatened, secluded suburbanites." "And so," he continues, "high T levels may not merely be responses to a violent environment; they may subsequently add to it in what becomes an increasingly violent, sexualized cycle." "It may be no accident that testosterone-soaked ghettos"—where is the evidence that whole *neighborhoods* are swimming in T?—"foster both high levels of crime and high levels of illegitimacy."

Where in the world is his understanding of other key factors for urban challenges? Here we find no mention of the likeliest contributors to crime and some pregnancies: unemployment, poverty, lack of recreation, lack of contraception, and underfunded schools.

"Word and system" are nowhere to be found in Sullivan's giddy ode to T. Indeed, "frustration" over inequality also fades by his essay's end. Sullivan concludes: "This doesn't mean that we shouldn't worry about individual cases of injustice; just that we shouldn't be shocked if gender inequality endures. And we should recognize that affirmative action for women (and men) in all arenas is an inherently utopian project." Not that he feels down or depressed about all this hopeless utopianism. Rather, since he stresses that we need a "new understanding of masculinity," he's cheered that "our increasing knowledge of testosterone suggests . . . a core understanding of what it is to be a man, for better and worse."

Or just for better. Stuck on what I call layer six of taking T—on self-report—Sullivan reveals a commitment to his layer-two gender fort. "For my part," he ends, "I'll keep injecting the Big T." "Apart from how great it makes me feel, I consider it no insult to anyone else's gender to celebrate the uniqueness of one's own." One man's celebration is another man's insult, for Sullivan next describes a world without the uniqueness of "his" hormone: "A world without the unruly, vulnerable, pioneering force of testosterone would be a fairer and calmer, but far grayer and duller place. It is certainly somewhere I would never want to live." (T *as* neighborhood?)

The last lines of "The He Hormone" deliver a punch(line) to those outside his gender fort: "I am perfectly happy to be a man, to feel things no woman will ever feel to the degree that I feel them, to experience the world in a way no woman ever has. And to do so without apology or shame."

"The Lie Hormone" says "The He Hormone" is telling a whopper. Trans man Evan Urquhart puts his self-report up against Sullivan's. Two years into his therapy on T (which he is content to just call testosterone), Urquhart considers Sullivan's claims to be "plain nonsense" in relation to Urquhart's own experience: "I can say with absolute certainty that the hormone didn't turn weakness to strength, passivity to ambition, or ambivalence to clarity."[18]

What's more, Urquhart presents himself as someone who has lived in two hormonal realms and can testify for himself—*and only for himself*—about those domains that

Sullivan says are so distinct. On the front of "horniness," Urquhart reports: "There's a common belief among men that male sexuality is a completely different animal than female sexuality." (Sullivan says as much. Recall his rats.)

"And this is understandable," Urquhart continues, "because they've never known anything different." By contrast, says Urquhart, as a trans man "I lived with a female hormonal balance for more than 30 years, and so I know that someone with estrogen and progesterone and a bit of testosterone is capable of feeling the exact same horniness. It's not like being in a different world, or even like being in a different neighborhood. It's horniness more often, or perhaps more likely to rise up unbidden. That's all."

One hears a voice when reading Urquhart that—no buts about it—is aware that taking T is a many-layered thing. He's finely attuned to the problem of studying the "psychological effects" of a drug so highly mythological in our culture. "Thoughts and feelings" are elusive study subjects—quite different from rats—and "our beliefs about what testosterone *might* do inevitably influence what we think it *has* done."

Consider a book that puts this all together, doing the highly difficult labor (so we don't have to) of studying the studies on T over decades. *Testosterone: An Unauthorized Biography*, by Rebecca Jordan-Young and Katrina Karkazis, wittily and learnedly takes the willing reader on a research ride that's hard to match. Its authors, more than any others on this topic, convey the range of "testosterone lore" to be found in *scholarship*. They nail the matter: "Of all [T's] powers . . . here's one [often] missed: T is a great storyteller"; the authorized "narrative sweeps away all kinds of details and smooths over contradictions."[19]

What arresting stories have indeed been told. The one they start with—because it's so preposterous and makes the point so memorably—is that of a French American physiologist, who, in 1889, to address his loss of strength due to age, gave himself injections of an "elixir made of testicular extracts from dogs and guinea pigs" (giving a whole new meaning to "hormonal cocktail," one could say). He of course reported a "radical change" in his well-being—in "just one day." Forearm strength, stamina, intellectual capacity, length of "jet of urine" (!), and ability to defecate were restored to youthful levels.

It would be amusing if this experiment didn't set a pattern in motion. Remarkably, it did. Here were the seeds of a quest for forms of ideal masculinity that, predictably, were early tangled up with racist goals for "racial improvement" in American men. The study that Sullivan cites about "inner-city youth" and "testosterone-soaked ghettos" is a flagrant example from the 1990s—one that the authors of *Testosterone* dismantle by restoring complication, context, and history.[20]

Restoring T's messiness is their stated mission.

One sees the need for their "unauthorized" tale of research intrigue, from the many years before T was chemically isolated in 1935 up through contemporary and racialized studies, such as the one Sullivan cites so blunderingly. Right from the get-go, we learn from Karkazis and Jordan-Young, scientists gathered data they considered "surprising," "paradoxical," and "disquieting." What was so unsettling? The discovery that "hormones were not sex-exclusive"—T did not *belong* to men—and the "actions [of hormones] were complementary rather than antagonistic." T, for example, is made in healthy ovaries that produce estrogen. That is, the hormones did not fit the plan to "explain sex differences" and justify the twoness of sex itself. T is not sex-specific.

So began a weakness the authors of *Testosterone* found was repeating through decades of research. Researchers "leapfrogged" over a first and definitive step: "meticulous documentation of everything that did and did not happen," with keen attention to "the myriad effects these hormones have." T is multiple, not singular, and context is nearly everything. "*Which* testosterone increases *which* aggression in *what* context?" That is the question the authors invite.

T, in the end, is everyone's story. But everyone's story is a layered story. And there are weirder stories surrounding masculinity.

The Strange Predicament of Boys' Masculinity

Talk about self-report.

A powerful new study reveals boys' dilemmas surrounding the towering ideal of masculinity, as *they* see it. The book is *Boys & Sex*, and author Peggy Orenstein is touted for "dar[ing] to do what so many of us are afraid of: actually ask boys about sex and then listen to what they had to say."[21] Self-report is the point. One hundred boys, ages sixteen to twenty-one, over two years, spoke with Orenstein about "masculinity, sex, and love"—along with "forces, seen and unseen, that shape them as men."[22]

Bewilderment and the flipping of binary power—as if your car flipped you upside down—are palpable surprises in Orenstein's study. You could say they're themes.

Boys are bewildered and so is she. She doesn't know what to make of what she's hearing or what to do about it. The titles of her essay in the *Atlantic*, where she usefully shorthands her study, show she's concerned. Her cover title reads: "What It Means to Be a Man: Boys Need a Better Answer than the One We're Giving Them." Then, on the inside, an intensified version: "The Miseducation of the American Boy: Why Boys Crack Up at Rape 'Jokes,' Think Having a Girlfriend Is 'Gay,' and Still Can't Cry—and Why We Need to Give Them New and Better Models of Masculinity."

"What it means to be a man" is exactly what her magazine essay doesn't answer. The bewilderment of boys runs so deep because they only know the brutal expectations of a gender—their own—that has turned on them. Counter to Sullivan's glory in T, these boys confess themselves as being *not* strong, *not* confident, and *not* not-depressed. Orenstein, moreover, great listener though she is, has no "better answer" and no "new . . . models of masculinity" to offer. Really, how could she? What she reveals is the molten core of gender's contradictions when the "ideals" of gender must be lived.

Ideals are brutal. You can't help but fail them, since they are ideal. That is, not real. If the ideal you fail, moreover, is the ideal that "you must not fail"—*this* is masculinity—you are going to be a failure, with consequences for everyone, including you.

Who is speaking in this study?

Orenstein says that "boys of all races" are represented in her study, but race is merely a ghost in the essay. (You think it will show, but it never becomes a part of her analysis.) Money is implied insofar as her study sticks "to those . . . in college or [are] college-bound, because like it or not, they're the ones most likely to set cultural norms." That is debatable. (Sports figures, musicians, and film celebrities all shape norms.) And are college boys setting gender norms or being set by them? No matter the other ninety-nine, one specific boy, taken as "typical," serves as the centerpiece of Orenstein's essay. He describes himself as a "typical tall white athletic" guy, with the goal of entering a military academy (think of "the soldier").

Orenstein immediately expresses surprise, since Cole (as she calls him) deems his girlfriend "'way smarter than I am,' a feminist, and a bedrock of emotional support." That's not a problem for Cole, as it happens. Rather, this is: "I needed to be a 'bro' and I didn't know how to do that." The word affects Cole—and Orenstein, too: "Whenever Cole uttered the word *bro*, he shifted his weight to take up more space, rocking back in his chair, and spoke from low in his throat, like he'd inhaled a lungful of weed. He grinned when I pointed that out. 'Yeah,' he said, 'that's part of it: seeming relaxed and never intrusive, yet somehow bringing out that aggression on the sports field. Because a 'bro'—he rocked back again—'is always, always an athlete.'"

Is Orenstein "word and system" attentive? She doesn't speak of systems. In fact, in the *Atlantic*, she never fills in who is giving boys inadequate answers and models with regard to masculinity. She speaks only of fathers and boys as spreading bad answers and faulty expectations. She does track words that wind around ideals. Tellingly, it's not that women are from Venus and men from Mars. It's that boys' ideals are channeling the distant 1950s. Orenstein reports: "When asked to describe the attributes of 'the ideal guy' . . . boys appeared to be harking back to 1955. Dominance. Aggression. Rugged good looks (with an emphasis on height). Sexual prowess. Stoicism. Athleticism. Wealth (at least some day)."

Something hides here. Something we know but perhaps forget. Dominance and aggression as a pair might be opposites, not companions. Those who have dominance need not aggress. Those who aggress signal lack of dominance. Aggression is a fear state. (This fear leaps to the level of systems. Aggressive security forces are said to act from their own—or the nation's—vulnerabilities. Run for the hills when power feels vulnerable.[23]) Orenstein's study bears this out, though she never states it.

Fear, insecurity, and outright weakness are the underbelly of the masculine ideal—since the ideal cannot be reached. Orenstein, likewise, makes this observation: "While following the conventional script may still bring social and professional rewards to boys and men, research shows that those who rigidly adhere to certain masculine norms are not only more likely to harass and bully others but *themselves* be victims of verbal or physical violence. . . . They are also less happy than other guys, with higher depression rates and fewer friends in whom they can confide."[24] This is the binary flip I've mentioned. The masculine ideal makes you docile to it, making you a "victim" of the ideal. (Of course, a caveat: don't dismiss the system of rewards gained here.)

Which is why boys are bewildered by their losses via masculinity. And why Orenstein, at a few junctures, is so

Fear, insecurity, and outright weakness are the underbelly of the masculine ideal—since the ideal cannot be reached.

puzzled—and a bit shocked. She is shocked by words. What boys can't say and what they have to say. Unsurprisingly, boys "routinely felt denied . . . the full spectrum of human expression." (Just think: that's *not* surprising, which is a little shocking.) Truly astounding is one boy's inability to cry, which leads him to stream three movies on the Holocaust just to emote when his parents divorce.

Then there's the locker room talk that cements certain words in place. Orenstein explains: "That question [about locker room words] always made . . . young men squirm. They'd rather talk about looking at porn, erectile dysfunction, premature ejaculation—*anything* else." (When Orenstein discussed her book on the radio, she said there was much she couldn't convey, given the censorship rules in place.[25]) Cole confesses: "We call each other pussies, bitches. We never say the N-word, though. That's going too far."[26] He continues: "One of my friends said we probably shouldn't say those words anymore . . . but what would we replace them with? We couldn't think of anything that bites as much. . . . [F]or some reason, *pussy* just works . . . just flows . . . [nothing else would] get inside my head the same way." Weird boy-loyalty to a word.

On the point of "fag"—a word the boys deploy but say they wouldn't use for "an actual homosexual"—Orenstein learns something that jars her understanding, something she considers truly "odd." Citing a study by C. J. Pascoe, Orenstein reports: "One of the more common reasons boys get tagged with *fag* is for acting romantically with a girl." "Which explains," writes Orenstein, "why one high-school junior told me that having a girlfriend was 'gay.'"

This nugget isn't news to gays and lesbians. Boys' sex with girls is for bonding with boys. Heterosex has a "homo" core: it ties you to your buddies. It becomes *talk*. Boys tell Orenstein: "the whole goal of going to a party is to hook up with girls then tell your guys about it"; "guys need to prove themselves to their guys" because the girl is just there "as a means for him to get off and to brag."

Fear sits here. Worries about skills; the danger of "a huge self-esteem suck"; not asking "what might feel better to [the girl], because that would have been admitting ignorance"; defining success as the boy's "own endurance," leading one boy to share how he always "glance[d] at the clock when he started penetration." The goal was to get past the point of "embarrassing." This kind of pressure "turns sex into a task—one I enjoy to a certain degree, but one where you're monitoring your performance rather than living in the moment."

Perhaps this pressure also fosters the aggression that signals lack of dominance. It's a reminder that docile bodies—docile to ideals—can sound (and be) violent. Orenstein registers a journalistic shudder: "No matter how often I heard it, the brutal language that even a conscientious young man like Nate [another of her subjects] used to describe sexual contact—*you hit that!*—always unnerved me. In mixed-sex groups, teenagers may talk about hooking up . . . but when guys are on their own, they nail, they pound, they bang, they smash, they hammer. They tap that ass, they tear her up." These boys are representative, Orenstein is saying, of the gender fort (to use my word).

She is struck by the fact that these behaviors are normative, not unusual. Revealing that she considers her default boy to be straight, white, middle-class-aspirational, and nondisabled, Orenstein summarizes her perplexity surrounding such a boy: "He may or may not post ever-escalating 'jokes' about women, or African Americans, or homosexuals, or disabled people on a group Snapchat. He may or may not send 'funny' texts to friends about 'girls who need to be raped,' or think it's hysterical to surprise a buddy with a meme in which a woman is being gagged by a penis, her mascara mixed with her tears. . . . Perfectly nice, bright, polite boys I interviewed had done one or another of these things." And there lies the problem for boys and those who love them—or just know them. Or don't know them.

"Hilarious," Orenstein comes to realize, is boys' word for blocking feelings, their own and those of others: "'Hilarious' is a haven, offering distance when something is inappropriate, confusing, depressing, unnerving, or horrifying; when something defies boys' ethics." It's even a way of stopping their "more compassionate response that could be read as unmasculine." She then concludes, showing but never quite recognizing the enormity of contradictions on display: "Boys may know when something is wrong; they may even know that true manhood—or maybe just common decency—compels them to speak up. Yet, too often, they fear that if they do, they'll . . . become the target of derision from other boys."

That's a bind, indeed. In being masculine (loyal, unfeeling, sticking with the boys), a boy becomes stereotypically unmasculine (cowardly, sheeplike). Cole cements this paradox: "To go up against that, to convince people that we don't need to put others down to lift ourselves up . . . I don't know. I would need to be some sort of superman." A superman, ironically, would fight masculinity—and be like a woman by showing compassion and common decency. This would take superhuman strength for a boy.

What a gender reveal this is. Orenstein's essay shows a queer predicament. A better masculinity can't be had if it would fit definitions of the "masculine." Put the problem this way: a better masculinity would seem like femininity—compassionate, emotionally flexible, expressive—where femininity would look like humanity—"common decency"—and both would be words for the same thing.

A question for later. Might masculinities become surface forms—matters of gesture, dress, and hair—not rooted in behaviors, exclusive definitions, and docile loyalties to a set ideal? As of yet, we have no answer.

Straight Women's Queerness

"Women," we should notice, have their own weirdness.

An index of this queerness is something called "chick lit." It has been humming for over two decades. You don't have to read it (I never have) to find it illuminates change for the word and people called "women." Again, the typicality of what's on display signals its whiteness—so the view is partial. Still, it's alerting and almost entertaining. To state it succinctly:

Shoe meets girl meets boy meets shoe. Shoes trump men. Men are shoes. Shoes are porn, of a charming sort. Sex is in the city. Austen's in the house. Love of Jane Austen is de rigueur. There's the "gorge factor" (the *author* must be gorgeous) with "toe cleavage" (did I mention shoes?)—and, defying feminism, the personal is no longer political: "It's just personal."[27]

And, of course, consumerist. Money-in-your-gender is on steroids here—the sense that you can buy your way to gender happiness in a world of things. Thus, if Orenstein's boys are bewildered, these newish women, *characters in fiction*, smack of an unrealistic joie de vivre: a well-heeled woman conquers all obstacles, we are asked to think. This is not a feminist critique of a system. Nor is it fear of what your gender asks of you. It's a woman's way of sitting with a muddle and not minding it. It's a telling fantasy. This we are shown by the "chickerati" as they offer literature that sounds like gum. (Chiclets, nonetheless, have been discontinued.)

We become aware of these matters through a study by Stephanie Harzewski, entitled *Chick Lit and Postfeminism*. Harzewski is a Virgil. With her voluminous knowledge of her underworld—one that is above ground, even all around us—she intends to school us in what has been read and seen by many women.

Think *The Nanny Diaries* next to *Pride and Prejudice*. No wonder there have been courses on chick lit in English departments and gender studies programs: for instance, a course at Texas A & M, "Flirting with the 'F-Word': Chick Lit, Feminism, and Postfeminism," and a class at Harvard, "The Romance: From Jane Austen to Chick Lit." Harzewski's own book could be called queer theory, since the massive oddities and clear contradictions of these straight protagonists (shoes over men, men as accessories) are so queer for all their normativity.

Normative strangeness can be magnetizing.

Orenstein as an attentive listener felt drawn into the drama of boys, though she recoiled from their "hilarity." Harzewski has felt the enjoyment of chick lit. She's a naughty Virgil: she is conducting a tour of her "sins" in all their ambivalence. "We have to work with this literature," she writes—since it's so informative—"but cannot become too friendly." For her "to devote a book to such fiction is to provoke accusations of succumbing to its contagious quality": "its humor, identification, delight, and fun."

What has caused this genre tells of gender change. Serial monogamy has given way to serial cohabitation that flexes and sways; marriage starts later, if it starts at all; there are "starter marriages" but fewer remarriages. The upshot for women is "singleton" lifestyles. Where are these factors best illuminated? In HBO's *Sex and the City*, starting in the late 1990s and kept alive in the subsequent movies (2008, 2010) and in reruns. (Plans for a 2018 sequel stalled over money.) What avid viewer can forget Carrie Bradshaw's "female dandyism," rooted in her shoes, leading to decisions—not to marry Aidan—based on such assessments as the ring "wasn't good" ("wrong ring, wrong guy"). (By contrast, the edgier, newer *Insecure*, which brings Black women into the fold of singleton focus, is too politically engaged for this genre.)

It is hard to argue against the conclusion that these fictions have "monumentally changed the representation of [white] single women" in the twenty-first century. And they are "postfeminist" (a term that originates in a 1919 women's literary manifesto, as Harzewski tells us). She continues: "While the market for the Harlequin romance [popular supermarket novels] exploded with the advent of second-wave feminism [in the 1970s], chick lit . . . has been frequently pointed to as evidence . . . of feminism's debilitation. The most popular image on chick lit book covers—high-heeled shoes with 'toe cleavage'—is an icon of postfeminism."

What are chick lit's strangest features and why are they postfeminist? The man and the woman, if you can believe it, are the oddest aspects, especially as a one-man-one-woman pair. The woman strays from one-man focus as she pursues sexual adventures, self-definition, work/life balance, self-improvement, climbing her professional (media) ladder, life in the city, and consumer luxuries. Perhaps more strikingly, the man is a "cipher" even when he's present: akin to the men "in bridal magazines," "the hero is a shadow . . . or background figure," since "men are not really valued as individuals as much as a means to a lifestyle, wedding, or in some cases beauty boost."

And, to boot, there's "almost nothing compelling about male sexual prowess" (one thinks of *Boys & Sex*). As a wife puts it in the novel *Elegance* by Kathleen Tessaro: "The truth is I don't want him to notice me, to cuddle me, to touch me, or to say how pretty I am. I just want him to leave me alone. After all that, I don't want to fuck him either." Therefore, says Harzewski, despite these novels' graphic sex scenes, there are only "minimal instances of genuine eroticism between men and women; men themselves are infrequently depicted as objects of desire."

Where does Eros go? Into luxury items. The utter strangeness of heterosexuality that we find in Orenstein's research takes a twist. Boys having sex with girls *for* boys was apparent in Orenstein's interviews with boys. Women having sex with men for shoes—no exaggeration—constitutes chick lit's very queer romance. Consumption becomes the heart of desire. Women seek commodities, it's suggested, that fulfill their drive toward celebrity life-styles and luxury weddings. Hence, chick lit's being designated "shopping-and-fucking feminism," "easy-to-swallow feminism," "user-friendly feminism."

Chick lit takes a cafeteria approach to feminist thought: it chooses what it needs and buys it for the moment. This consumerist approach to ideas and political commitments means that heterosexuality cannot be separated from "business-based diction and economic considerations." (There's your Jane Austen coming to America?) That is very normative, indeed. There is no interest in income disparity other than one's own. Therefore, chick lit's central theme is "professional ascendancy," "leav[ing] the impression that every media employee will become a columnist, a best-selling author, or TV personality—and while she is still under thirty-five."

Self-help, self-care, "romances of the self." The man has all but disappeared. The women aren't concerned.

Is this a departure from feminist thought? Simply put, postfeminism is a cloudy matter. Chick lit questions the family, marriage, and men as answers to women's problems. At the same time, it eschews the f-word. (In fact, Harzewski tells us, "feminism" seemed to grace the "do-not-use list" for *Sex and the City*, despite the show's love of freewheeling speech.)

Still, postfeminism does love empowerment—just not "public political action" or collective protest or what they imply (complaint, dowdiness, shrillness, evidently). Nor does postfeminism critique oppressive systems, preferring instead more of a straddling of the (un)conventional positions offered women. Postfeminism, then, "negotiates the tensions" between feminism and the thing called "femininity." Or, if one prefers, Harzewski offers a less pretty picture when she cites the take of Diane Negra and Yvonne Tasker, who say that postfeminism "tends to confuse self-interest with individuality and elevates consumption as a strategy for healing those dissatisfactions that might alternately be understood in terms of social ills and discontents."

Gender norms for women—that affect us all—make it hard to get ourselves unstuck from matters adhering to chick lit. The sometimes-terrible joys of consumerism beg a reckoning with our gender. Thus, it may be that what scares observers and political types is the thought that issues sticking to chick lit stick (like discontinued gum) to you and me.

Gender Exuberance, Racial Oppression (Racial Exuberance, Gender Oppression)

Now think encounters between *gays* and shoes. Shoes speak the beauty of Black men strutting in spaces their city barely knows exist.

We will find a paradigm in this swagger. Joyful expressions of gendered beauty are made more layered when the racialization of gender is so evident. When race and gender palpably cross. Of course, they're always crossing—always intersecting—but the "colorblind" force of whiteness is formidable.[28] Whiteness gets to hide. Not confess itself. That's how chick lit, boys, and dolls (to take a few examples) appear as topics lightly treating race. And how people-of-color exuberance seems to have to—or perhaps want to—grasp the play of racialization.

As for oppression, it is doubly winding around the dynamics of race and gender that are never separable from each other. Three distinct contexts—Black gay ballrooms, Latinas' realm of gesture, and Asian dance performance—render the queerness of gender in ways not widely apparent. That in itself tells us just how blinkered whiteness makes "the public."

Visibility operates diversely in these contexts. A closet is generally considered out of view. A place a person harbors themselves for private safety. So we have seen in the long and complicated history of closeting for gays and lesbians.

Counter to this privacy, Black gay men have made a closet from a ballroom—quite a *social* closet. A place to be seen. A place to display and perform and become. However ephemerally. However routinely.[29] So we discover in *Butch Queens Up in Pumps: Gender, Performance, and Ballroom Culture in Detroit* by Marlon Bailey.

A ballroom is a no-space, in the sense of a utopian space that does not exist beyond its walls. It's a space for dreaming, since it has a twilight existence at night. This doesn't mean it's static or floating or unchanging. (Bailey's loving study is from 2013.) Surely, like gender, Ballroom culture is on the move.[30] Still . . .

Whatever it is, it's a place for pumps—for getting up in pumps—making the shoe a pivot for action. The action is both a dressing-up and coming-out—all inside a closet. Participants, specifically, come out into "families" devised as "houses" named for designers who design pumps. House of Dior, House of Ford . . . The luxury item surfaces, now becoming a force for making families.

And though this culture with its ballrooms and families has flourished in Manhattan, it hasn't owed its beauties to the city's gay neighborhoods. (It began in Harlem.) Poor and working-class queers of color do not "have" a neighborhood, even though they are Black or Latinx like their fellow neighbors. Their danger is constantly all around them, save for the ballroom, which is a "multidimensional world" that may exist for some of its denizens strictly online—in chat rooms, on websites, YouTube, or Facebook.[31]

What about cities being in our gender? Detroit's specificities remind us that a city's uniqueness matters for raced and gendered lives. From boomtown to rust-town, Detroit—and its Black population most intensely—has suffered through spectacular deindustrialization (where union-busting has gone hand in hand with immense segregation). One of the poorest populations in the country, African Americans in Detroit had seen their unemployment climb to 17 percent during Bailey's research; 48 percent of the city's children had fallen into poverty; and eight hundred LGBT youth had found themselves homeless every day on city streets.

Here's where something as micro as gestures—the range of gendered gestural performance propped by clothing and music and runways—may save lives, as dramatic as that sounds. Gendered survival exists in this setting. So do out and out *creations* of genders. Indeed, for readers of Bailey's book, Ballroom culture, apart from the city, inside the city, informed by the city, becomes quite discernible as "cultural labor." Ballroom gays are making something—something sustaining and a bit spectacular—that includes their gender. Bailey names three labors: "individual and communal self-fashioning"; the "construction of a minoritarian community"; and creative, alternative "response[s] to the HIV/AIDS crisis."

Gendered survival exists in this setting. So do out and out *creations* of genders.

This is not the self-care bubble of chick lit, to put it mildly. Working on your gender is collective work. You construct your gender for yourself and others. Ambitiously, Black gay men here fashion—fashion is the word—a gender *system*. Sexuality enters in, showing again how often the two go hand in hand. This is less freeform than one might picture, though it is spirited and inventive. Also revealing of the pressure of norms. (Might Mount Holyoke nod in recognition?) Here are Ballroom genders, with Bailey's explanations:

Butch Queens Up in Drag (gay men who perform in drag but do not take hormones and do not live as women)

Femme Queens (transgender women or MTF [Male to Female] at various stages of gender transition)

Butches (transgender men or FTM [Female to Male] at various stages of gender transition . . . or masculine lesbians or females appearing as men irrespective of their sexuality)

Women (biological females who live as women and are lesbian, straight identified, or queer)

Men/Trade (biological males who live as men, are very masculine, and are straight identified or nongay identified)

Butch Queens (biological males who live and identify as gay or bisexual men and are or can be masculine, hypermasculine—as in thug masculinity—or very feminine)

Notably, this system of six distinct genders—fluid as a system, fixed for individuals—shows a paradoxical *expansion* of *fixity*.

The point is to "learn the performance norms" governing Ballroom competition categories and master them so powerfully that, states a flyer, "your mother can't tell; your father can't tell." You pass safely on Detroit's city streets. Safety is the proof of one's gestural prowess. Or, as Bailey puts it, "the central goal . . . is to be undifferentiated from the rest of Black working-class people in the urban space."

Because the goal is blending, the enactment of this system involves a series of performance roles, such as (what are called) Realness categories. "Executive Realness" and "Schoolboy Realness" are two examples. In the "Executive Realness" category, folks who are decidedly not bankers or CEOs cannily know that money's in our gender, since the goal here is "to perform heteromasculinity for 'Wall Street,' to be seen as a gender-normative businessman." To be "real," says Bailey, is "to minimize or eliminate any sign of deviation" from the norms that rule these roles. You know you're not a businessman, but you can look the part.

Somehow you know that looking like a businessman has been central to the men who get to be one.[32]

The ballroom is a lab, a machine, a closet where the Ballroom denizens *show* how gendered passing is made—and pleasurably unmade. Bailey paints absorbing scenes. Among them, he renders the "Realness with a Twist" competition category—a Ballroom performance that is a rehearsal for "life in the . . . world."[33]

The Twist goes like this: "The performer, who is almost always a Butch queen [gay or bisexual], displays both extremes of the masculine-to-feminine spectrum in one performance." Thus, a performance of Thug Realness, gestured and embodied to the beat of hip-hop on the runway, stops on a dime. When the DJ plays "The Ha Dance," by Masters at Work, signaling that voguing should now commence, the performer "queens out." (There's a lovely phrase, sounding like a peacock fanning its tail.) That is to say, "he performs vogue femme, the style of 'soft and cunt'" (terms of respect). His gestures turn elegant, fluid, and feminine. His gender change, moreover, changes the reading of his sexuality. The performer's transformation from masculine to feminine takes him from "unclockable"—not gay-appearing—to a state of "clockable"—marking him as exuberantly gay.

All of which is pretty queer, indeed. From this extraordinary sex in the city, we can see gender as gestural and joyful. Also as tinted by a range of fleeting and emotion-laden moments.

Consult your own gender and you'll find a mixture of system-driven meanings and bodily flickerings. You'll find gestures. The way you signal emphasis, wave, or touch your hair. Gesture doesn't reduce to systems—the way my lover specifically gestures for me to kiss her is all her own—but systems like gender and race play complexly in our motions. Juana María Rodríguez goes deeply into gestures in her study *Sexual Futures, Queer Gestures, and Other Latina Longings*.

The gesture rendered in flesh is her focus. Yes, it's repeatable. That's how it *means*. But the body's singularity gets involved. And there's relationality (as with a gesture beckoning a kiss).

"Gestures hang and fall," writes Rodríguez.[34] "They register the . . . effort of communication." However private in a setting, they're "relational." They connect people, and "they form connections between different parts of our bodies." (For instance, hand and lips.) "They cite other gestures." (A masculine stroking of the chin may be citing an image from a movie or the gesture of a brother.) And they're prosthetic: "They extend the reach of the self into the space between us; they bring into being the possibility of a 'we.'"

Gestures queer gender. Queers and Latinas distinctly greet each other via an "over-the-top" allure fashioned by their gestural fancies. (Think Cardi B and Jonathan Van Ness—the Afro-Latina rapper and the *Queer Eye* maven—and you're there.) "We swish too much and speak too loudly," Rodríguez explains. And the "amplified . . . rhythms of our moving bodies signal—through the glut of expression—our surplus sexuality." Latinas and queers *enjoy* "our bodies betraying . . . our intentions to exceed the norms of proper . . . containment." (If you've seen Cardi B twerking in a tiger suit, this point's made.) In fact, Rodríguez delightedly cites a study from 1966, conducted by a scholar of intercultural communication. Having counted "the number of times couples in different national locations touched each other as they sat in cafes across the globe," he announced Puerto Ricans as the lucky winners, since they touched each other "180 times in the span of one hour."

There's an underside to gesture.

If gestures are inventive, Rodríguez cautions, "they also make public the imprint of our past." (They bespeak our gender fort.) Here she has in mind how gestures act as archive, storing signs of "social and cultural laws" in our most personal gesticulations. (Cultural law: a man must never, ever drop his wrist if manliness is what he intends to signal.) For this reason, our most cherished fantasies may be wed to gestures that carry abjection.

Racial migration is the scene Rodríguez presents to work this out. "I'm Your Puppet," a cabaret show from 2007, enacts a troubling scene of a Latina's "sexual violation at the U.S.–Mexico border."[35] At one point in the performance, a border agent slowly strips the Latina, shifting the audience's expectation from a cabaret-style female striptease (controlled by the performer) to something more debasing. "The audience at this point," Rodríguez explains, "is at a loss, not knowing whether to cheer at her increasing exposure, or boo at the staged violation." Almost fully stripped, the woman appears to gain US entry but "once across the threshold, she is nevertheless detained and led offstage."

The gestures of this gendered scene are familiar. They are recognizable because they are repeatable. They map onto findings by the ACLU about reported cases (over two hundred in just four years) of sexual violations in detention facilities for Mexican immigrants.[36] But this performance—staged as burlesque, with the border agent played by a Native butch woman—is "marked as a brown-on-brown, butch-on-femme interface of erotic power" that elicits anxiety, titillation, political discomfort, repulsion, outrage, and arousal.

Put this alongside a scene from BorderBangers.com ("Where hot Latinas fuck or get deported!")—subscription porn, if you haven't guessed. Rodríguez wants to get at what we deem obscene. And she wants to locate unusual elements in narrative scripts and the gestures they require. Rodríguez is setting a trap for her reader. She's showing our *normative* views as obscenity. What's more indecent: standard porno images of sexual acts or the economic violence of government power on a woman's body? Do we also find the "placement of Latinas in the racially gendered service economy" to be offensive? These points lead Rodríguez to a BorderBangers scene that in its yearning gestures and soft, hushed tones carries subtle tenderness, even intimacy, on the back of racially gendered abjection. Shards of these fantasies, Rodríguez is telling us, live quite palpably in our gender archive: "Over time (or in an instant), they start to form part of the narratives we take to bed or screen or club or altar."

If we ask ourselves, we really do know this. The gender archive is a gesture archive. Fantasy rides the back of gestures.

Imagine a baton toss at this juncture to a certain boy—a certain kind of boy—and to the fantasy surrounding such a boy. The current figure of the "Asian houseboy"—a male domestic fulfilling all needs—has his own story and archive of allure. Gendered performance and nuanced sexuality appear here, too. To trace this fantasy, one will need knowledge of the strange seduction that was played out by the "white man" and "native boy" for over a century of contact in colonial spaces. American fantasies have deep roots.

Perhaps you have heard of the figure of the "rice queen." Should you not be up on him, Eng-Beng Lim, in his *Brown Boys and Rice Queens: Spellbinding Performance in the Asias*, will bring you up to speed. (Having grown up as a queer boy in Singapore, Lim didn't know this figure either.) Essentially, the rice queen is "a gay Asiaphile" of European-American background "whose primary attraction" is the "nubile . . . brown boy."[37]

Much like an old colonial photograph that ends up as a postcard, these lived relations carry on with import and to bold effect (the houseboy trope and the category "rice queen"). Yet, these afterlives are anything but still. They appear now, as they did then, as a gendered exuberance of music, dance, and gesture. *A House in Bali*, a 2010 opera performed at Brooklyn's Academy of Music, is Lim's Exhibit A. The opera emerges from a memoir of this title that appeared in 1947 by Colin McPhee, who happens to be known as an originator of the field of "world music." (This is not your garden variety rice queen.)

The opera itself—a "'multimedia phantasmagoria of Eastern and Western music'"—with a "sixteen-member Balinese" ensemble with Balinese singers—has a boy at its core. As Lim tells it from attending the performance: "While music played a big role in the show, the most fascinating discovery that evening for the audience was the character of Sampih, an eight-year-old Balinese dancing boy who was the love object of the thirty-one-year-old

Canadian musician Colin McPhee"; "in fact, there was so much enthusiasm for him that the actor playing the part joined the curtain call to a literal gasp in the auditorium."

Self-confessing, Lim relates: "There was something palpably seductive and 'wrong' about the spectacle to be clapping so hard, though I could not say what it was just yet"; "I was spellbound and sick, euphoric and catatonic." All of which leads Lim to ask about the audience: "Was the queer content simply disavowed [by them] . . . for a mesmerizing Balinese experience"? Was this music-magic, with this dazzling boy, a symbol of something so much larger? Was a voluminous fantasy at stake?

These are not moralizing questions for Lim. He's not playing conservative gotcha. Like Rodríguez, he is scouting the public, "normal" reception of erotic modes that otherwise might seem wrong and strange by normative measures. Lim finds a paradigm at play in these matters. That is, "the Sampih-Colin . . . love story is not exceptional." Lim's Exhibit B: examples of this coupling are abundantly found in the lives and literary works of André Gide, Paul Bowles, William Burroughs, Lawrence Durrell, Gustave Flaubert, T. E. Lawrence, Edmund Backhouse, John Moray Stuart-Young, and E. M. Forster. A literary who's who of authors.

Why does this matter? It proves a large dynamic. Lim finds a pattern in this man/boy pairing that suggests the sexy servitude of Asian performance on the world stage and American scene. That's an immense gendered legacy with its man/boy lover core. (You can bet a US audience would disavow those roots.) Still, Lim asserts with persuasive force that Sampih as McPhee's "muse, son, adoptee, houseboy, trophy dancer, and lover" reveals a stance baked into the cake of our viewership of Balinese performance, if we ourselves are not Balinese—maybe even if we are.

Consider this colonial postcard come to life:

> Their wet brown skins shone in the sun as they danced up and down in the ecstasy of nakedness. They were completely wild, agile, and delirious as a treeful of monkeys. . . . When we reached land this naked, dripping youngster and I stood facing one another. He was perhaps eight, underfed and skimpy, with eyes too large for his face, daring and slightly mocking. I offered him a cigarette, but he suddenly took fright and was off into the water before I could say a word.

This is from McPhee. Lim takes these sentiments as signs of a spell. The spell itself indicates the "allegory of Asia infantilized and emasculated as a nubile brown boy," whose end isn't pretty. Sampih is murdered at age twenty-eight. The native boy as figure is made to dance into the twenty-first century nonetheless.

That's the rub of
gender. It runs a range
of scales—from
continental size to
the size of a child. And
it's always racialized.

Lest we forget the role of gesture, there is *kecak*. "Widely known to tourists as the 'monkey dance,' *kecak* features a large Balinese male chorus performing a polyrhythmic chant with synchronized gestures and throbbing bodies in a multilayered circular structure"—a dance that was "often performed with traditions of ritual possession" and solidified Bali's "exoticism as a tourist spectacle."

Again, the plot thickens around a man and boy(s). Spellbound Walter Spies (a German expat), employing "a host of nameless boys" in Bali as "houseboys," photographic "models," and "lovers," captures with his camera in the 1920's and 1930's what so entrances him. Boys in motion, boys in repose, boys peering out from masks and leaves. And Lim is our guide for this queering of the ethnographic gaze on the native boy, who himself might be "playing with Spies."

This two-way play, never equal, never static, never free from mockery, never free from dare, emerges inside Lim's examinations. Dense, tangled, illicit, (un)deniable: this tale's elements of spellbinding love, felt by individual colonizing men *and* American theater audiences, make the brown boy an agent, a target, a houseboy, a symbol.

That's the rub of gender. It runs a range of scales—from continental size to the size of a child. And it's always racialized.

How in the world did it come to be?

WHEN WAS GENDER?

Short take:
Gender's history beckons. It's not dry. After all, it's yours. Something that happened in human history "gave" you gender. Now, from the surface of your body to your brain, gender's gone to work on you, even if you've spurned it.

Do you know the history of the concept "gender"? There's this man . . . In fact, there are two. One founds gender. The other gynecology. We will get to both—one at the start, one at the end. But if you're suspecting these histories can't be simple, can't be the product of two individuals, you'd be right. Quite the adventure, quite the spread of actors—leading to the politics of Black Lives Matter and queer migration movements—takes place here.

Settle in for history—since it is yours.

How Does It Happen that You Are Gendered?

Intersex and transgender children, Black female slaves, and a raft of feminists hold the answer. You owe your gendering, however you regard it, to these specific groups.

You might well imagine we've always had gender. (It might hark from the dawn of time?) Or you might be savvy and know it's historical but find it hard to pinpoint. You are not alone. Gender has a history and it's more recent than many people realize.

Many expert thinkers are likely to imagine that feminist writers invented gender. Many *contemporary* feminists may think so. Indeed, why wouldn't they? It would be logical—and, frankly, appealing—to believe that women seeking equality would champion a concept that implies change. Whereas sex is given, the story often goes—you have certain genitals by which you are sexed—gender is behavior and social conditioning and learned ways of being that we can unlearn, unmake, undo. Gender is distinctive from sex, it's been claimed.

Gender is our hero for everyone's sake?

Seventies' and '80s' feminists are certainly part of gender's story. In ways more intriguing than just described. But a different history—of intersexed and transgender children—what was done to them—tells a starker tale. (Intersex children, as mentioned earlier, are born with features—genitals, hormones, gonads, or chromosomes—

that do not "fit the typical definitions of male or female" bodies.[1] Transgender children do not feel right in their sex assigned at birth.) This bleaker history happens over decades (five, to be exact), culminating in gender's creation as a concept in the 1950s, so as, some would say, *to save the binary division of sex* (sex as male and female) from its own collapse.

Gender *saves* sex? Gender is a traitor, not a superhero? If this sounds pernicious, there is more to come. The founding of gynecology is equally astonishing. First, to the birth of gender itself.

Money Made Gender

The moral of the story: beware when science wants you.

Gender gets made from children's having something science found valuable. Jules Gill-Peterson, in her recent book *Histories of the Transgender Child*, tells us how it all went down. It's not that medicine made trans children. It's that children's sense of themselves as something-other-than-what-they-were-assigned got *taken up* by medicine—across five decades of medical research (1900–1950)—before the crowning of the thing called gender.

This means the newness and now-ness of "trans" kids as a phenomenon is a "myth." They are not recent—not as you might think. They have a history under the eyes of doctors and parents, as Gill-Peterson carefully shows.[2] Just as crucially, they didn't need medicine in order to grasp their determined wishes.

What happened, then?

Intersex children and transgender children (not yet named as such) held something that would prove quite dear to US science in the twentieth century: the capacity to be transformed by medicine. Indeed, these children became "living laboratories."[3] They were deemed "plastic" enough to be changed—first through surgeries, later by hormones—often in the name of "correction." Their "peculiar" suffering could be studied, treated, and corrected. If they disagreed with their bodies—didn't feel like the sex they were assigned—disagreed with their genitals— agreement could be fashioned. Medically, surgically.

If they were white. The children not selected, rarely presented, never sought out for medical treatment (however highly torturous) were children of color.

They did not hold value in the same way. Decades of eugenic thought and aims—beliefs about the backwardness and unsuitability for future promise of Black persons—were deeply in the ferment of these research settings. Besides, we learn, "the few black intersex children and families" seen in the clinics and institute contexts (at Johns Hopkins, quite specifically) "were regarded by staff as more 'difficult,' combative, irrational, and . . . disposable." Thus, as Gill-Peterson powerfully claims, "the medicalization of trans life," right from the beginning, "fundamentally racialized it."

This is where gender takes center stage. A crisis was brewing. Due to this cadre of certain white children who didn't fit the measures of binary sex, biology and medicine were facing a cataclysm. Those most knowledgeable understood the plastic nature of the body—along with the possibility of its not matching itself at all levels. They of all observers feared that the proof for binary sex was crumbling before them, given that a series of "predictors" for male or female status didn't reliably predict at all. Chromosomes were no sure ground whatsoever; having testes or ovaries didn't do it; even hormones, for complicated reasons, didn't prove predictive; and genitals or secondary sex characteristics could clearly go awry.

Gender to the rescue. In the most circular but interesting of ways, gender is invented to shore up sex. Scholar John Money is the king of the inventors. King of the *interpreters*. For gender's own story is not a fly-by-night creation by a singular person, waving a wand—though there's a powerful man in this story. The story of gender is a crucial gathering. A veritable crisis of interpretation. Then, a turning point.

The story to be gleaned from reading Gill-Peterson can be put this way. Money, with his colleagues, largely rolled 1950's norms over scientific data so as to defend against what that data showed. Without enough interest, in the

Gender's own story is not a fly-by-night creation by a singular person, waving a wand—though there's a powerful man in this story. The story of gender is a crucial gathering. A veritable crisis of interpretation. Then, a turning point.

deepest sense, to listen to children or even inform them about their treatment, Money embraced changeability with one hand while grasping at fixity with the other.

Here's how he did it. To defeat the crisis that humans "were naturally . . . sexually indeterminate," Money argued that children are actually born plastic and remain plastic *for a certain time*. Hence, you can use surgery and hormones to "correct" their bodies and "finish" their genitals, if their genitals prove ambiguous. After this time (around eighteen months), children must grow in *developmental* channels, "*either* male or female." Why must they do so? In order "to prevent" their suffering from "social stigma" or psychological distress (from their not complying with their gender fort). These two channels for children's development—only two—are what Money then called "gender."

There's your circle. *Society*, ignorant of medical research, makes a stigma out of something our bodies do quite naturally: *not* conform to a sexual binary. Thus, society's enforced binary corrects a problem of its own making. And medicine complies, against its own research. Quite unlike later feminist notions—that gender is dynamic, changing, changeable, and capable of undermining social norms and their stigmatizing ways—Money's "gender"—gender's founding moment—argued for something much more fixed and stigmatizing, all while purporting to sidestep stigma.

Society, ignorant of medical research, makes a stigma out of something our bodies do quite naturally: *not* conform to a sexual binary. Thus, society's enforced binary corrects a problem of its own making. And medicine complies, against its own research.

Money's not alone in tangled thought. Many different feminists have tried their hand at parsing sex/gender, from the 1960s to the present day. Among the questions implicitly tackled: Should we seek to equalize the terms *man* and *woman*? But how could they be equalized without our changing their meanings so completely that they cease to mean? Would this be the point? (*Fog* them to death.) Or should we open up positive meanings, powerful meanings, for the term *woman* so that it starts to receive its due? (Largely, it has served as a photographic negative of the term *man*.) How can "woman" come into its own if it's locked in dynamic tension with "man"? Can we crash the system of sex and gender by multiplying terms? (Think of Mount Holyoke and the Ballroom gays.) Or can we only reveal the comedy, the theater, of gender as required performance? (Lil Nas X has something to say.) *What if the category woman itself excludes many women?*

Reading feminists, we learn how these terms bedeviled thinkers who fought inequalities and gendered precarities. As an opening salvo to where we need to go, next comes a question that will later make sense.

Gender Quiz

Ask yourself what the following have in common:

A Black man's marching with the sign "I Am a Man"

A picture of a woman's labial lips

A car at an intersection hit from two directions

Whether or not this question finds you stumped, down the line it will clarify how gender muddies sex.

Marriage in Your Gender

Was your mother or her mother trafficked?

If this query jars you, or seems like it comes from the wild blue yonder, the next stage in gender's history will explain it, even answer it.

There has been said to be trafficking in marriage. It is a trafficking in human bodies—even though slavery isn't its focus (Black female slaves are this chapter's culmination). Asking for a hand seems unambitious. Even slightly creepy. Yet it's been common. A hand, an aisle, a father, a groom. "Asking a father" for his daughter's "hand in marriage" was a household phrase for the longest time in US contexts. "Who gives this woman to be married to this man?" was standardly asked at US weddings (still may be)—and the father, having walked the bride down the aisle, would "give away the bride" (that was the actual language) to the groom.

But *trafficking* in marriage?

Marriage, indeed, is the focal point of the essay "The Traffic in Women: Notes on the 'Political Economy' of Sex." Sex is also its central topic, as the title tells us. Sex in two senses: the thing called a person's biological sex and sexual acts that bodies do. The author is feminist Gayle Rubin, and the piece itself was a blockbuster essay in 1975. Important to mark (it's hard to miss) is that Rubin used the term "woman" in that period to designate something like a *class* of people—people called females—whom she regarded as oppressed in a highly similar way. That way was marriage—and sex with men. This was not a popular thought in the '70s. Even today, it would not win a spot on *Good Morning America*.

Rubin called this trafficking an everyday system. "A sex/gender system" with such familiarity, you might not recognize its purpose and its patterns.[4] With deceptive calm, Rubin described them. She was inquiring how a "female" person gets made into "an oppressed woman." Central to this "making" was the transformation of "biological sexuality"—which she saw as capable of taking any number of expressions, forms, and pleasures—into fixed "products of human activity."

Perhaps you hear an echo of Karl Marx here. Raw material is turned by activity into products. (Leather, for example, via human labor, becomes a sexy shoe.) That's no mistake. Rubin is saying that the raw material of female sexuality is being made into a kind of product for men's satisfaction. Marx, however, just didn't get it. He didn't account for sex, Rubin says. Sigmund Freud did.

Freud to the rescue? In a certain sense. Rubin explains: "By contrast [with Marx], in the maps of social reality drawn by Freud . . . there is a deep recognition of the place of sexuality in society, and of the profound differences between the social experience of men and women." Marx failed to analyze human sex. He also didn't theorize women's domestic labor in their homes. Since no wage was paid, it wasn't seen as *work*. Women weren't workers in Marx's classic sense.

Marksman-like, Rubin makes sex her target. As she puts it tellingly: "Any society will have some systematic ways to deal with sex, gender, and babies, but it is important . . . to maintain a distinction between the human capacity and necessity to create a sexual world and the empirically oppressive ways in which sexual worlds have been organized."

Bottom line: things don't have to be this way. Sexual worlds could be created differently.

Rubin, however, has to press forward with the sexual world that's right in front of her. It involves (what she calls) "the traffic in women," with its echoes of slavery (but no specific mention of African American women or American bondage). To bring marriage into trafficking, Rubin explains (as she draws on anthropologist Claude

Lévi-Strauss) that "marriages are a most basic form of gift exchange, in which it is women who are the most precious of gifts."

Why, precisely, are women gifted? For the sake of the (good old) incest taboo, which requires that marriages go outside families so as to make ties with other family units. It's not too bald to say: In many US families, women were given by men to men. Strange normativity strikes again. Another big instance of how, historically, gender has been queer for everyone. (Those not marrying were still shaped by it. Marriage made you "single" in '75 if you didn't partake. Vestiges of these dynamics remain.[5]) And it might get stranger the more you think about it. Rubin puts it this way: "If it is women who are being transacted, then it is the men who give and take them who are linked, the woman being a conduit of a relationship rather than a partner to it."[6]

Men marry men in marrying women? Orenstein's boys' having sex with girls for the sake of boys' relations with boys returns to view and makes more "sense." Here is an indirect reply to Sullivan's testosterone thesis. In Rubin's wording: "The 'exchange of women' is a . . . powerful concept. . . . in that it places the oppression of women within social systems, rather than in biology."

A racial dimension unfolds right here at the crossroads of biology and social oppression. If you haven't guessed it, a Black man's marching (say, in the '60s or '70s or beyond) with the sign "I Am a Man" means that male genitals (and

Men marry men in marrying women?

Strange normativity strikes again.

sex assigned at birth) do not guarantee the gendering they point to. "I Am a Man" surely means "I Am Human"—that is clear as day—but it also demonstrates that male genitals do not automatically get the humanity accorded men. This gendered fact has striking consequences for Black men's unemployment; African American female-headed households; Black gendering writ large; and the forms of masculinity that presume control of capital and control of women. Rubin doesn't go here.

Rubin heads to heterosexuality. The points she makes are powerful because she starts to dig at the roots of the presumed sexual differences between men and women. Even if bodies have different genital configurations, why should labor be so divided along these lines? (Rubin, of course, spanked Marx on this question.) Lévi-Strauss answers and Rubin pounces to stress his reply. The "purpose" of labor differences between men and women, says Lévi-Strauss, is to "insure the union of men and women by making the smallest viable economic unit"—*the marital household*—"contain at least one man, one woman." The division of labor, by this logic, is a "device" to produce heterosexuality. To enthrone it. Make it money.

Nefariously, in Rubin's view, dividing labor by sex is a "taboo against the sameness of men and women, a taboo [that] divid[es] the sexes into two mutually exclusive categories, a taboo which exacerbates the biological differences between the sexes and thereby *creates* gender."

Rubin, as if she were sniffing out Money, sees the crafting of the thing called gender as a way to prop up the notion that there are two sexes that exclude each other. Put differently, she says: "Exclusive gender identity is the suppression of natural similarities." Put differently again (think of Sullivan, who happens to be gay): "If biological and hormonal imperatives were as overwhelming as popular mythology would have them, it would hardly be necessary to insure heterosexual unions by means of economic interdependency."

There is more to Rubin's take. But a different feminist takes us more deeply into genitals ("into" is the word), so we turn to her and the question of lips.

Two Lips Touching

When you think about your genitals—just how often do you think about them?—the fate-shaping force of genitals is obvious.

Concepts of genitals were shaping talk of sex in that formative time of 1970s feminist thought. Genitals remain so stubbornly central to *gender*'s story as a result. Did anyone approach them from a novel angle, you might wonder, helping us raise more searching questions?

I recall a panoply of colored, gripping forms. Some were bluish-pink; some deep black; some raw-ish red;

textures were unique. One shiny surface gave way to raised speckles; another led into the crinkled canyons of elongated folds. Spectacular variation—disorientation—left my head swimming. *Near the Big Chakra* was searching all right.

Such are my memories (undoubtedly creative) of this documentary from the 1970s—one I viewed in Utah in 1987 at an art cinema named (I'm not kidding) Cinema in Your Face. One lone synopsis of the film's plot reads: "Extreme close-ups of 38 vulvas, aged three months to fifty-six years, including two blacks, one half-oriental girl [*sic!*], two lesbians, one prostitute, two adult virgins, three mothers to be, three grandmothers, four women menstruating, one girl with gonorrhea (learned just days after the shoot), a woman who learned she had uterine cancer three weeks after the shoot, and a lot of mothers." Quite a description, mixing kinds of categories. Popping right up in this synopsis, moreover, is racially prejudicial language (there it is, so casually). Differently striking in this entry is the comment: "The Glide Methodist Church's education division, which specialized in community service related to sexuality and pregnancy, produced the film, despite the director's male colleagues finding the concept unsavory."[7]

Indeed, this wordless film leaves all to ponder the savoriness of genitals that are rarely given this visual weight. Something occluded was emphasized as hidden, while it became an ocular feast. I don't recall my thoughts, but ponder I did.

What about words? What is there to say about genital form(s) so little displayed? Leave it to the French to create a book title that stops you in your tracks. *This Sex Which Is Not One*—is this a declaration? a complaint? a fact?—was how Luce Irigaray, famous French feminist, titled the translation of her 1977 book, which followed on the heels of her *Speculum of the Other Woman* (1974).[8] Psychoanalyst, philosopher, and linguist, Irigaray wrote abstractly and elliptically.

But her point was blunt. "Woman" as a sex is actually nothing. "She" is not one. Not a sex at all. "She" doesn't rise to the level of a sex in the so-called binary. "Man" is a sex and "she" only mirrors him back to himself by being whatever "he" is not. He is rational, she is emotional; he is strong, she is soft; he is stoic, she is compassionate . . . (He's a bro, she's a pussy . . . This would sound so reductively absurd if it didn't happen to be "true" definitionally. "Masculine" and "feminine" have to be distinct and mutually exclusive, it's been thought, for their meanings to hold. Orenstein's boys are anxiously baffled because it is hard to live these definitions. No one does, no one can.)

Or try it this way. Not only is she ("woman") "not one," she doesn't "have one." With no penis—that is how she's seen and named at birth—she becomes a "hole" or a kind of "envelope" (a penis turned inside out, say embryologists) to sheath him, fit him, and be filled by him.[9] Genitally, also, she is his inverse.

Is she? Really? If she were a body in her own right, if one looked through the speculum anew, if one touched on her bodily folds, might a different view emerge? She would not be *one*. She, the singular body of a woman, would be many communicating zones: clitoris, vagina, nipples, skin, labial lips, and other unnamed erogenous sources. You're right, says Irigaray: this sex is not one.

Quite on purpose, Irigaray chooses lips as the place to plant her flag. Almost everyone does have lips. They're not unique to women, since they're found on faces. Some human beings have genital lips and do a range of things with them. (Irigaray doesn't address trans bodies. A trans man might find pleasure in his lips or use them creatively. Or, not at all.)

Why such reverence for (genital) lips?

Slyly, Irigaray can make many points with them. She can dethrone the penis as the hinge on which sex hangs—do you have one or not? "Woman" does not reduce to penis-lacking. Nor is her organ an inferior penis (the little hooded clitoris) or the vagina (a hole for his filling). Rather, Irigaray wants to make an unseen body seen— seen *as* unseen. She would like to underscore how rarely women's bodies are actually explored (outside of a medical, experimental scene that has had its own disasters, as we'll see). This new seeing of bodily form might allow bodies to be creative, liquid forms that can be unformed, deformed, and re-formed, outside authoritative, set parameters. Perhaps they'd reform the concept of "form," making it more seductively opaque to terms at hand. (*What is this surface? How is it becoming? How spelunk its depths? How preserve its pleasures?*[10])

All child bodies, we must remember, lose direct material access to themselves when they enter language. Many sensations start to be gathered under a sign-assigned-due-to-genitals (that word-cone, that beginning of the fort). The bodies of boys, along with those of girls, suffer this loss. It's just that boy-bodies get as their cone a powerful word. Their word says: you haven't lost a thing; you've got it, bro; tap that ass!; hilarious.

All of which takes us to the space between the lips. Their lack of closure. Alluringly, Irigaray makes the *apartness* of one lip from another the lips' essential feature, biologically, symbolically. Because each lip is split from the other—there's a blessed space between them—they can be separate enough to touch each other; they can be open to words and other pleasures; they can speak the sexiness of failing fully to close upon each other.

If you can believe it, the genital lips are a model for sexual relating and desire in Irigaray's writings. *Failing* and *lacking* are the very drivers of sexual pleasure: happy failure to overtake your other; joyful failure to solve their opacity; letting your lacking them (not quite having them) shape your burn for them. This (hot) lacking is *shared between* bodies.

"Man" and "woman," then, are not really sexes. (Stay with me here.) They are two positions. Two distinct orientations toward desire. "Man" designates a drive toward fulfillment and satiation, even though fulfillment is always ahead of him and never enough. (There must be an endless supply of women, since accumulation—counting them—is key. Orenstein gives boy-evidence for this.) "Woman" names a different stance, for pleasure's sake: "nearness," not domination, is the goal. (Think of two lips touching. Never do they fuse.)[11]

In what *looks like* a "lesbian" tryst, Irigaray envisions a person *positioned* as a "woman" approaching another person so positioned, thus crafting erotic exchanges around the crack of desire between them. Whatever their assigned or even chosen sex, and whatever their play of genders might be (at the level of dress, mannerisms, sex acts), the crucial factor in this exchange is their stance on lack. Do they make forms of incompletion (nonpossession, loneliness, separateness, sorrow, pain, failure) and impossibility (non-knowledge, non-closure) central to their bliss and their sexual nearness to each other?

There is even a critique of capitalism (!) found at the lips. Irigaray, like Rubin, calls keen attention to women's domestic and sexual labor performed for men—how it is both unwaged and unseen. But her biggest move is to criticize extreme goal-driven desire, such as "masculine" and capitalist thrusts together display. Irigaray calls this an "all but one" mentality: I have them all—all but one. I have them all—women, possessions, dollars, lands—aside from one. I need that, too (that final one).

Masculine capitalist desire *needs a lack always ahead of it* ("all but one") in order to pursue its goals and pleasures. Irigaray, by contrast, would place this driving approach in the space *between (not ahead of)* desiring bodies. Sex, for Irigaray, demands the attempt to keep closing the gap while nurturing the lack, infinitely approaching one's other/lover with deep curiosity but never reaching them. Thus, she would steal the dynamism, the excitement, the restlessness of capitalism, while reconceiving its central aim.

This is just a taste of Irigaray. More of her, however, from that crucial time, would not take you into racialized gender. "Woman" for her was *nearly* a class. But the implications of whiteness were her blinkeredness, for all her critique of what lies unexamined. And the implications of "woman" as a racially divided term remained untouched by her.

At the River: Black Feminist Lesbians Speak

This sex which is not one, indeed.

A group of Black feminist lesbians had—still have—something to say that raises this matter to the third or umpteenth power. They were busy approaching them-selves, their words, their labor, and their own activities in the 1970s. (Black Lives Matter—today's most central activist group combating antiBlackness—springs in large measure from these roots.[12])

You could say they, too, were working to make the unseen seen and seen *as* unseen. They were literally mak-ing a statement. Among their activities, they gathered up words to confront their cone-words and theorize, from the depths of their experience, the impossible position of their lives. Their proclamation was the Combahee River Collective Statement (CRCS).[13] It is now widely credited as the start of grasping racialized gender in the lives of those wearing "Black," "woman," "lesbian," "working-class," "poor," and many other signs upon their bodies. How could they be *one*—a singular, already-accounted-for sex—when they weren't recognized as the confluence of signs they had been living?

Confluence is an apt word here. It should conjure riv-ers. The name of the CRCS is taken from an action at a river. At the Combahee River, Harriet Tubman, known for her work on the Underground Railroad, became the only woman in US history to plan and lead a military campaign. Her action, in 1863, freed more than 750 slaves. Should you be someone who doesn't know this fact, ask why this event has been unknown to you.

Also, consider confluence as metaphor. (Its definition: "the junction of two rivers, especially rivers of approximately equal width."[14]) Race and sex. Antiracism, antisexism. *Black* and *woman*: how could Combahee's activists choose between these terms that were attached to them at birth? And how could Black feminist lesbians even reduce to "Black" and "woman" if they acknowledged their sexuality, itself suspect and shocking in mainstream '70s culture, never mind their class, which made these women themselves suspect that capitalist dreams did not include them?

Theirs was "not a mixed cake."

So said Demita Frazier, a founding member of the CRC. She meant that the group had to make its meanings and aims "from scratch."[15] They were creating organizing structures alongside "friendship networks, community and a rich Black women's culture where none had existed before." From which we glean that there was an innovative, pleasurable, luxuriant side to their laboring over their unseen-ness, despite their evident "life and death struggle." (These tones saturate Barbara Smith's essay "Doing It from Scratch: The Challenge of Black Lesbian Organizing," with its title's nod to Frazier's phrase.) There was organizing, and there was writing. To act, they thought.

Three bold statements inside their Statement put their thinking into words: "We realize that the only people who care enough about us to work consistently for our liberation are us. Our politics evolve from a healthy love for ourselves, our sisters and our community which allows us to continue our struggle in the world."[16]

Their work was positively autoerotic. They must touch upon themselves. You might not think it would have to be so. Wouldn't the multiple-source oppression of Black women cause more alarm and thus more care? It didn't work that way. Their complex positioning put Black feminist lesbians at risk of no one caring to think that hard (or love that hard) to grasp their "double jeopardy." Were they being treated like an algebraic X no one would solve for? Did their specificity not get taken up because their *value* didn't register?

They were the "very bottom," said the Statement, "of the American capitalist economy." Money was everywhere in their differently gendered sex—and they knew it. They worked for wages *and* did unwaged work at home—quite the double-whammy—and were still the nadir of the economic scale. (Keeanga-Yamahtta Taylor, in a book that contains the Statement and interviews its authors—Barbara Smith, Beverly Smith, and Demita Frazier—tells us that, in 2017, when Taylor was writing to commemorate the Statement's fortieth anniversary, Black women "make up 25 percent of the poor, compared to Black men, who are 18 percent; and to white women, who make up 10 percent of the poor.")

Rather than critiquing Marx, the CRC aimed to "extend" him. Workplace organizing sat right next to picketing for health care and founding a rape crisis center in a neighborhood. Here was a sense of extension, indeed: "If Black women were free, it would mean that everyone else would have to be free since our freedom would necessitate the destruction of all the systems of oppression."

By touching on themselves, they were freeing everyone. Fighting for their freedoms—to live, love, and share in the profits of their own labor—truly basic aims—they would free all others. A show-stopping claim. It demanded reckoning. (Its legacy today is profoundly apparent and gathering steam: All lives cannot matter until Black Lives Matter.)

It did not hold sway. The Statement proclaims: "Feminism is, nevertheless, very threatening to the majority of Black people because it calls into question some of the most basic assumptions about our existence, i.e., that sex should be a determinant of power relationships." Crucially and strikingly, the CRC's Black feminist lesbians did not seek to separate themselves from larger Black communities or Black men, specifically. They remained in solidarity with other Black people taking up Black struggles. But here came *sex* to split Black feminists from anyone believing in the "misguided notion" of "biological maleness" as that which "makes [men] what they are."

You have to wonder if their lives as "lesbians" made them question what is natural or biological. Presumably, they felt perfectly natural when being deemed unnatural, so the thought of "natural" might have been flawed to them? Of course, having seen how the notion of "natural" white superiority was preposterous—was based on melanin in one's skin—they might have concluded that another superiority ("biological maleness") was about cultural power, not biology.

Black feminist lesbians, then, had these windows onto the pamphlets of some Black nationalists in that time of ferment. The Statement quotes from one (which traffics in claims that Rubin was confronting):

> It is only reasonable that the man be the head of
> the house.... Women cannot do the same things
> as men—they are made by nature to function
> differently. Equality of men and women is something
> that cannot happen even in the abstract world....
> The value of men and women can be seen in the value
> of gold and silver—they are not equal but both have
> great value.... [M]en and women are a complement
> to each other because there is no house/family
> without a man and his wife. Both are essential to the
> development of any life.

The Statement did not use the word "gender" to counter these claims, but it was crafting gender in the face of sex. It was saying no to a difference in value set by genitals. And by skin tone.

The CRC also could not abide by flaws in the stance of white feminists: their (sometimes stunning) lack of curiosity about Black lesbians and other Black people; their wrong belief in the "primacy of gender." The fact that reproductive rights activism emphasized abortion rights above all else showed the inability of white feminists to grasp the importance of freedom from sterilization for Black and brown women (and, much clearer now, for a range of women institutionalized with disabilities).

"This is not a 'guilt trip'"; "It's a fact trip," said Barbara Smith in a different essay.[17] And if white women were tired of being reminded of racism? "Imagine how much more tired we are of constantly experiencing it." Besides, says Smith: "Racism distorts and lessens your own lives as white women . . . [so] it is very definitely your issue."

Who would care to heed these words?

So much was held in the spareness and elegance of the word "care." And so much would come from the CRC phrase "interlocking oppressions." That's how "the intersection" surfaced as a metaphor. It became key to Black feminist thought of the early 1990s, after it was named in 1989, and then indispensable to all kinds of thinking on racialized gender and sexuality.

Then and Now: At the Intersection

A car at an intersection is the simple concept. It gets hit from multiple directions—or gets hit and hits another car.

If the car's occupants end up injured, which hit harmed them?

Yes, this is a metaphor. But Kimberlé Crenshaw, a Black legal scholar, was making a critical point about the law in 1989 when she coined the term "intersectionality."[18] It wasn't abstract. Black women's workplace discrimination might be due to racism, sexism, class oppression, or some combination of all three systems. That's because systems of social inequality obviously "overlap and cross each other, creating complex intersections" where a person's injuries may occur from several simultaneous impacts.[19]

Crenshaw would be the first to say—indeed, has said—that "intersectionality" was "a lived reality before it was a term."[20] The CRC had been living this reality and speaking to its force. The intersection metaphor gave it both a visual and a new word to hold it all together. One could thus see how the damage of a crash was not simply additive (racism + sexism = a set sum of injuries). Nor could the impacts be deemed parallel or analogous (racism and sexism as equally injurious in all contexts). Being called "Black" + "woman" (+ "lesbian" + "disabled," let's say) was a compound matter that was hard to calculate, never mind describe.

But describe one must. The CRC had used the phrase "identity politics." These days, "identity" can sound quite personal, individual, and chosen. A kind of "tunnel vision," say its critics. This was not the gist of the CRC's use. Their understanding was something much closer to the mantra I've suggested: "word and system." For the CRC and, later, for Crenshaw and other thinkers (Patricia Hill Collins and Beverly Guy-Sheftall[21]), identities were the *products* of oppressive systems (and, I would add, words put upon us). Speaking, then, from the place of one's identities meant speaking up and out of these words and the systems attached to them. These fateful words, however liquid they could be, were congealed forms with meanings that had hardened.

Not to be missed: the state has the power to give and take identities. The birth certificate is just the start. The marriage certificate is another layer. And citizenship is a state-controlled naming of major import. In fact, says scholar Shuddhabrata Sengupta, "the Eurocentric white Judeo-Christian male heterosexual" "pretends that everything other than what he holds dear is an identity."[22] So, identity politics are identity struggles.

There is a mystery to every combination. How distinct words combine on a body moving through the world is not completely evident, though history and laws and stereotypes and self-proclaimed cultural meanings are at play. We are back to layered entities (recall those baby sexlayers) that may conflict or disagree with each other—on the body of a person. As Sengupta poses in a striking question: "Are you the white working-class woman, perhaps a single mother, who is herself a victim of insidious sexism within the military and within working-class subcultures, who nevertheless becomes a willing enforcer of the apparatus of humiliation in the Abu Ghraib prison?" Or: "Are you the African American GI in Iraq, sucked into the poverty draft at home and face to face with the anger of a subject population that considers you to be a brutal enforcer of an occupying army?"

Here's a trial for politics. If intersections are so interactive and sometimes contradictory, does intersectionality risk too much complexity and thus unorganized, ill-defined goals or lack of common cause or even paralysis? Not necessarily. Systems and words are massively communal; living them can be movingly solitary. We should fathom both of these scales.

At the scale of movements, we can consider queer migration matters. From Karma Chávez, we learn of a "strategic intersectionality" (the phrase comes from scholar Marie-Claire Belleau[23]). In her *Queer Migration Politics: Activist Rhetoric and Coalitional Possibilities*, Chávez tells how undocumented youth purposely use LGBT tactics as a "coalitional gesture" that builds solidarity and *points to* civil rights withheld from US denizens who are not citizens.[24]

This convergence hails from 2010 when the "DREAM Act 21," "a group of self-identified undocumented youth," staged a series of campaigns. Chief among their tactics lay a letter-writing action directed at then-President Obama, modeled on one undertaken by the OutServe-

Servicemembers Legal Defense Network, who were agitating for gays to serve openly in the US military. More dramatically, migrant youth activists made an equally direct appropriation of LGBT tactics when they announced (again in 2010) a National Coming Out of the Shadows Day. A day to openly declare themselves "undocumented and unafraid."

This was a knowing appropriation.

"Coming out," says Chávez, became a key strategy of the migrant youth movement and indeed "catapult[ed] queer migrants" (as it happens, they accounted for a "disproportionate number" of migrant youth activists) into national movement leaders. And here we see the upsides and downsides of this strategic political intersection between "queer" and "migrant." For one, you can't miss the overlap and breakaway between the terms "closet" and "shadows." (The latter has none of the positive privilege of space for privacy, spiritual reflection, and valuables-storage that the former holds.) Second, dangers and false liberties attach to un-concealing oneself in saying, "I am gay"/"I am undocumented." One comes out *into* the law (as Oscar Wilde famously learned long ago) and into the arms of the state's and the general public's definitions. *They*, in large measure, say who you are.

Besides, there's a normative thrust to coming out: "a desire to belong to a community and alter that community's boundaries" so as to be included. Can there be an edgier blade—not "asking to belong to the system as it is" but seeking instead "to radically change it"? Either way, of course, one embraces a troubling "logic of legal citizenship" that confirms nation-states.

There's the pitfall. Queer activism, Chávez knows well, teaches a stunningly resonant lesson. (Think of AIDS activism, as well as that "on behalf of poor, homeless, drug-using, gender-nonconforming, sex-working queers, especially queers of color.") "Criminalized populations . . . can expect little more than further criminalization" if they go head-on against the law and state. This is the lesson Stonewall teaches, despite "gay" "progress" for certain (moneyed) queers.

For those wearing both words on their bodies—"migrant" and "queer"—or "DACA" and "queer"—the intersectional identity of "undocuqueer" can create a sense of personal limbo, even as one might organize around it. Jesus Cisneros, in his published interviews with undocuqueer immigrants, cites "Patricia," a twenty-five-year-old "DACA recipient":

> I saw how my immigration status was being
> discussed in one space, and then we were told,
> don't talk about your sexual identity. . . . And in
> LGBT spaces, I'm like, why are we not talking about
> these other identities that folks have, whether
> it's their immigration status or whether it's their

socioeconomic background, that limits them to have resources—in terms of what it means to be LGBT?[25]

"I was actually confronted with like, what am I?" adds Ester, twenty-six years old, trans, and DACA-mented. Another undocuqueer activist points out: "I think that if there wasn't an undocuqueer movement, I don't think there would be a push back like against the criminalization of our trans brothers and sisters." And being undocuqueer for "Daniel" meant stepping away from the DREAMer script. Cisneros reports: "For Daniel, this [DREAMer] rhetoric reinforced class-based suppression . . . as it absolved the blame from children but continued to criminalize parents and other non-student identities."

This is why radical counter-DREAM activists, such as Herrera Soto and others, warn "inclusion will always be premised upon others' exclusion from the possibility for a livable life."[26] A more moving coalitional politics requires counter-DREAMing and concocting a nonnation entity, a country-less collective, trying to grasp worlds-coming-to-be.

Jetting back in time, we can hear these struggles—escape and exile—cravings for inclusion that enact exclusions—in the writings of Chicana lesbian activist Cherríe Moraga (composed around the time of the CRC Statement). Moraga is writing at the solitary scale of systems lived inside one life.

The act of uncloseting, even unburying one's own self, can promise exile. Moraga gauged escape—into her experimental sexual life—by her exile from her mother. Hers is a version of the labyrinthine, subtle snaking of a racial sign through one's gender—and, in her case, through a brown mother ghosting her life.

Call this a browning of Freudian theory: returning to your mother who signifies a color you are destined to relate to, fitfully, unconsciously. Moraga's story pivots on the axis of her mother, in *Loving in the War Years*. Moraga is a moon to her brother's sun. Pale and "exiled into the darkness of the night," she states, she is "writing in exile."[27] She is like the Aztec moon, she says, "severed into pieces in the war against her brother," he who as a male receives her mother's love unreservedly, just as she gives it without measure.

Moraga's moon metaphor renders her exile—into both whiteness and her desires. She is fair-skinned, passing for white, knowing the "danger of putting . . . 'lesbian' and 'Chicana' together on the same page." No wonder Moraga, at twelve years old, dreams of lying in a hospital bed: "[My] breasts are large and ample. And below my stomach, I see my own cock, wildly shooting menstrual blood totally out of control. The image of the hermaphrodite." She is "bleached and beached," as she says succinctly. And she is betrayed by the very woman—her Chicana mother, married to an anglo—who has strangely inspired her love of women by withholding motherly love from Moraga. In a poem, she asks: "What kind of lover have you made me, mother / *so in love* / with what is left / unrequited"; "the gash sewn back into a snarl / would last for years."

Paradoxically, in love with an illiterate, dark-skinned, wounding mother, Moraga becomes an assimilating, light-skinned, educated writer, whose mother-infused woman-love poignantly returns her to Chicana contexts: "When I finally lifted the lid to my lesbianism, a profound connection with my mother reawakened in me," alongside "empathy for my mother's oppression," since "in this country, lesbianism"—not just illiteracy—is "poverty." So, she writes, "I am a white girl gone brown to the color of my mother speaking for her"; "I long to enter [her] like a temple."

The play of ranging scales is where our bodies sit. We can organize around them. Doing so, we think beyond the what and when of "gender."

Now we conclude with a frightening episode occurring more than fifty years before the term was coined.

Gynecology's Raw Undoings

Something foretold that a man would make gender. A white man, at that. (A man named Money, to complete the circle.) Another white man had already made the field that would study women's genitals, inside and out.

This is the bookend to gender's story. The founding of gynecology is its own sick twist in the history of gender and sex as jointly troubled. To understand how, we encounter claims from scholars Hortense Spillers and C. Riley Snorton, who make "Black gender" a confrontation of "sex" *and* "gender."

Spillers has famously claimed that slavery *ungendered* bodies otherwise marked as men and women, mothers and fathers. Slavery turned bodies and people into "flesh": unspecified material.[28] Raw material. Ungendered forms to be shipped across the seas.

It's not hard to see how Spillers grounds this point. The transatlantic journey that we call the Middle Passage, bringing "the slaves" to American soil, "culturally 'unmade'" them. They were being ripped from their cultures as they sailed. "Under these conditions," Spillers asserts, "one is neither female, nor male"—both are only "*quantities*." The effects for Black gender are monumental.

Snorton picks up on this famous claim. In *Black on Both Sides: A Racial History of Trans Identity*, Snorton puts dynamics of the trans-Atlantic (back) into "trans." Normative gendering was never on the table for Black slave women. Yet their bodies were crossroads for "sex." Snorton shows how the field of gynecology—the field that studies and treats "female" genitals—founded itself on the flesh of "chattel women."[29] Black women's bodies were the scene of experiments addressing gynecological disease.

Hortense Spillers has famously claimed that slavery turned bodies and people into "flesh": unspecified material. Raw material. Ungendered forms to be shipped across the seas.

Yet they birthed a field that could not encompass them, since they could never be gendered as "women"—"normal" white women—no matter the surgeries performed upon them. None of this stopped James Marion Sims, the field's founding "father," from becoming the president of the American Medical Association in 1876 and the president of the American Gynecological Association in 1880. A first-name-only slave, Anarcha, is even referred to as the field's "mother."

Here is the flipside to what Gill-Peterson cites for trans and intersex children. In the latter story, largely white children end up tortured into "normal" status. In the tale that Snorton tells, Black female slaves—no less tortured by medical procedures—become the "raw materials" for making "women's medicine" (as a new field), from which Black women "were excluded as women." The promise of "being made again a normal woman" through surgeries on their genital disease "would not be available" to these women slaves, who didn't have the rights or status of "woman."

To say this story is gruesome is to understate what is hard to hear. The disease Sims addressed—vesicovaginal fistula, caused by "a massive crush injury" to the "tissues of the pelvis"—was so disturbing in its symptoms—a "continuous involuntary discharge of urine"—that many white women would not go to doctors, or even killed themselves, lest they be seen as "objects of disgust." Enslaved

Black women, by contrast, were lent by their owners to Sims and Sims's promised "care" (unanesthetized procedures, numberless surgeries, bold examinations of their naked bodies, excruciating pain), showing that "enslavement was a necessary condition for [Sims's] test subjects," who upon their cure were *returned* to their slavers.

Here women's "sex"—what can be learned about "female genitals"—is grounded in the properties of "ungendered" flesh.

So, if white women and Black (ungendered) women were so extremely different, were they more opposite of one another than they were opposite of white men and Black men? What a messy matter. Are the notions of "opposite sex" and "same sex" problems at their core? If so, the status of "homo" and "hetero" comes undone.

Thus, a pointed question: Who's my opposite?

WHO'S MY OPPOSITE?

Short take:
Let's consider calmly whether we still cut babies in half. As you scratch your head, consider the sword that performs the cutting. It's a simple phrase.

"Opposites attract."

Baby-cutting. Swords. Surely, I'm being melodramatic? No one takes a sabre to a baby—but we sex it. (Plato, we learn, has thoughts on cutting.) The time has arrived to grasp this phrase. To view it perhaps as a terror trap. True, there's a breezy use of this phrase. Popular psychology asks us to ponder, "How are you different from your lover's personality?" (She is quiet, I am loud; she is calming, I am angsty . . . Opposites attract.) That's not my focus.

My point is that this phrase has caused such havoc while it makes no sense. (Repeat, as you fall on your pillow at night: "It makes no sense.") Genitals are not opposites of each other; people aren't opposites based on their genitals. Hetero/homo makes no sense. (If people aren't opposites, nor are they "the same.")

Making no sense has not stopped the damage attached to this phrase. So, we will visit: why I'm not my girlfriend; sex in the restroom; Black Panther quandaries; the paradox of *Fight Club*; and something heart-arresting. Black, Indigenous, and other people of color, including, palpably, Asian Americans—gay, straight, whatever—might well sense that their histories strike a blow to "opposites attract." At such cost . . . to Black, Indigenous, and other people of color.

This racial story is key to what I tell.

Who Coined the Phrase?

"Opposites attract." This has been a saying since . . . I don't know when. No one seems to know, including the singer Paula Abdul, whose hit-song single from 1990 was titled with this phrase.

The *idea* goes back to Plato.

Picture elite Athenian men—philosophers and playwrights—enjoying each other's cerebral company, surrounded by appealing sensual pleasures. (The pleasure-field contains eroticized women and attractive younger men.) Grapes must abound. Someone tells a story of the origins of love.

This is a scene from Plato's *Symposium*. The speaker of the tale is the playwright Aristophanes, and his little myth gives visual form to "opposites attract"—but also more. *The Symposium*, considered one of the "great books" of the Western intellectual tradition, gives its readers a threesome, not a twosome, which has effects on notions of attraction.

Three different roly-poly forms roamed the earth in the time of Zeus, as the story goes. Each was a spherical human volume—four legs, four hands, one head, two faces. (You may be sensing where this leads.) One volume was male-bodied with male faces; one was fully female; one was half and half. And though you might think these spherical forms would just be playful, rolling about, the gods found them threatening. Rather than destroy them, Zeus debilitated them. He cut them each in half. This swift severing left each half in search of its other, "longing" to once again "grow into one."[1]

A crazy little myth.

Or it would be comical, if we didn't still prune babies. We cut children in half when we sex them ("boy" or "girl"), since we conceive them as half of a human sex spectrum. Also half of a sexual pairing. They must seek their other (lost) half in love. The search can now be legally homo or hetero—we've caught up to Plato—but, for a long time, it could just be hetero.

Just one problem. Race and class and gender variations sound absent from this sexing. That can't be. In the US, they're intensely present, have always been present. Homosexuality, then, to take one of Plato's pairings, *can't* be a search for one's lost half—the other half of a same-sex duo. That's too simple. Sexuality, whether it be homo or hetero, does not reduce to *sex* in either of its senses (sex assigned at birth or sexual acts). Other major factors are always in play.

Take it from me, a self-confessed seeker of same-sex sex. Except I don't believe in any such thing.

I Am Not My Girlfriend

Consider these lines from my (anti-)memoir, *Making Out*:

> I am not my girlfriend. We are not the same. Our genitals are different. Mine are not hers, so they're not the same. We use them differently; their use is not the same. I do things to pleasure her a man could also do—and if she closed her eyes, she might think I were he. If she always closed her eyes, she'd never know if he were me.
>
> We've had different ways of coming to our "sameness," a sameness so undone by the ways we've come to it. The crucial point is this: we are

each strangers to the word "lesbian" and the word estranges us each from ourselves. I was female-assigned at birth, though I was a boy (I could only guess) mistaken for a girl. (I was in deep disagreement with my genitals.) And though I was, I felt, the ultimate straight boy seeking normally feminine girls, I became a "lesbian" against my will—in accord with my desire.

As for my girlfriend, she grew up, she felt, "normally" feminine as a rural Mormon raised in rural Utah. In her twenties, after her male fiancé died, after she didn't become a missionary, after she walked across the U.S. for nuclear disarmament, she met lesbians and wished she could be one, since they were rakish enough—and smart. But, she figured, she wasn't a lesbian.

Long story short: I didn't want the word but was pierced by it; she quite wanted it but didn't think she'd gain it. We are homo-*white*, if we're homo-anything. Alike in racial background, not in our gendering or class formation or histories of attraction.[2]

Have we ever had, then, a two-sex system, "man" and "woman," in this country's history? Since this nation's founding, we have consciously, often legally, had *at least* a six-sex system (with more sexes beyond the thirteen colonies): white woman, white man, Black woman, Black man, Native woman, Native man . . . This becomes more stunning the more one considers it, raising the question: who is my "opposite," my "opposite sex"? There are no opposites with six or more sexes.

A problem thus looms: *Are there no such entities* as men and women—those bold opposites? Our bathrooms say there are.

Sex in the Restroom

Every time you visit a restroom marked with the sign "Men" or "Women," you are being sexed. This is not surprising. The sign says it all. We're used to this effect.

Less well known is that we're being ordered by nineteenth-century norms. Expressly, we are sorted at the bathroom door by the old assumptions that women are a weaker, more vulnerable, if more moral, sex that needs protecting. The history of the bathroom tells us so. "Separate and *un*equal" is its message. Or, if you prefer, "opposites attract." The restroom tells you whom you should fear—if you're a "woman"—and whom you should desire. They are both one and the same.

Restroom scholars are currently excavating public building codes; architecture layouts; rationales for restrooms divided by sex. This in a time when restrooms are

Since this nation's founding, we have consciously, often legally, had *at least* a six-sex system.

Expressly, we are sorted at the bathroom door by the old assumptions that women are a weaker, more vulnerable, sex that needs protecting. The history of the bathroom tells us so.

changing—becoming all-gendered, even ungendered. And, simultaneously, when the public restroom, in its old modes, is being reconfirmed. Then, unconfirmed. North Carolina's "HB 2" was enacted by its state legislature not long ago (2016). And has been repealed. It stated in part that all multiple-user bathrooms and changing facilities in public schools "be designated for and used only by students based on their biological sex."[3] Gavin Grimm, a teenage trans boy, battled similar dictates in Virginia—and prevailed.[4] "Gender" beat "sex." Gender trumped genitals.

Terry Kogan, a legal scholar, helps reveal the history that grounds these issues. Kogan reminds us that "separating public restrooms by sex" is relatively new in human history.[5] Insofar as it's been so, "a sexist vision that pervaded American culture" made it so. Kogan is referring to the "separate spheres ideology" central to nineteenth-century US thought. Citing David Shi, Kogan gives us a crystallized version:

> During the nineteenth century, the genteel elite—as well as an emergent middle class—developed an ardent faith in the civilizing power of moral women. Females were widely assumed to be endowed with greater moral sensibility and religious inclinations than men. Such pedestaled notions of women helped nourish a powerful "cult of domesticity." . . . As the more complex economy of the nineteenth century

matured, economic production was increasingly separated from the home, and the absence of men who left to work long hours in the city transformed the middle-class home into a "separate sphere" governed by mothers.

Money was definitely in their gender. Class priorities, job arrangements, and the marital divisions of labor that Rubin fingered all emerge here. Notice as well that when *governing* mothers stepped a toe outside their homes, they became weak. The city was their kryptonite.

The lure of consumer goods—chick lit would be pleased—was a reason women ventured into cities. Governing women needed to spend. But where would they "rest"? And how do it separately? Kogan finds an "ingenious" solution in architecture history. "Beginning in the 1810s," Kogan tells us, "architects began cordoning off ladies-only parlor spaces in public buildings and on modes of transportation." In 1829, Boston's Tremont House Hotel was among the first hotels to do such cordoning. Women came into the building via a separate side entrance. Inside, they found "exclusive parlor spaces" just for them. For dining, for drawing, for receiving each other—separate from men.

Tremont House Hotel achieved another first. It was also "the first major public building in America to bring plumbing indoors." Intriguingly, its eight water closets for the public were not sex-segregated. Why? Kogan speculates that they were intended for men, not women, given the assumption "that women's presence in public places would be limited." Twenty years later, when toilets moved indoors on a larger scale, they began appearing next to the separate parlor spaces in public buildings, making them "the first sex-separated indoor toilets in America."

So ends the tale of toilets.

Well, it doesn't. It has continued to this very day, backed by laws and building codes. And there was a period, not to be forgotten, that confirmed our country's sense of there being many sexes. The Southern Standard Building Code, in 1945, began its separate but unequal toilet requirements for Black and white men and women. (The date is telling: after World War II, when Blacks had served the nation as segregated soldiers, they would be thanked with new segregations. These segregations were clearly a response to increasing integrations—among them racial, sexual "mixings.") Stated the code: "Where negroes and whites are accommodated there shall be separate toilet facilities provided for the former, marked plainly 'For Negroes Only.'" Race was being treated to the practices of sex. Here were at least four marked sexes.

Sex-separation, sex-segregation. We are not out of segregated times. Sex is still a segregating force. Yet there's something new. A pathbreaking push called the *Stalled!* Project, co-led by Kogan, trans scholar Susan Stryker, and architectural scholar Joel Sanders, has recently successfully lobbied the International Code Council. Starting in 2021, the International Building Code will "allow for (but not require) all-gender multiuser restrooms in public buildings." Segregation and integration now overlap in the world of the restroom.

Which leaves a sexual thread hanging. Since nineteenth-century norms shaped our public restrooms, was something left unsaid in all this separation? Did men and women need separate toilets publicly, since these sexes must entwine privately? Culturally, we are ceasing to feel so certain about how "sex" and "gender identity," even "sexual orientation," converge in the restroom (someone next to you may be desiring you . . .). We only seem sure that race has no place in discussions of the bathroom.

The restroom has been busy providing false certainties. Other contemplations haven't been so confident. Sometimes it just isn't easy to tell who is opposite of whom, even when believing "opposites attract."

When You Can't Tell Your Sameness from Your Difference

Two intriguing touchstones for attraction-trouble are Eldridge Cleaver's memoir *Soul on Ice* (from 1968) and the still famous, much-taught *Fight Club* (1999). Each is its own bible of masculinity.

Cleaver's is one of the most fraught texts you can read on the racialization of gender. Writing at a time of Black Panther politics—he was their minister of information, after all—Cleaver published *Soul on Ice* three years after the infamous *Moynihan Report* on "the Negro Family" of 1965. Not to be forgotten, that report by liberal Democrat Daniel Patrick Moynihan (with friends like these, as the saying goes, who needs enemies?) described the "Negro" family as a "tangle of pathology" because of Black folks' female-headed homes.[6] The report is now known for its matriarchy thesis: strong Black women make Black men weak; something is upside down in Black gender.

Cleaver takes a different tack. He considers both Black partners strong. Which is the *problem*. For attraction.

Before we hear Cleaver stating his worry, it's crucial to note that a fuller understanding of Black Panther politics is now at last reaching a broader public audience. Their breakfast program, their push for education, their community care, and their refusal to accept the police brutality widely practiced on Black communities—all express the Panther platform. *And* some members—Cleaver most of all—were flummoxed by how to embrace their masculinity, given its racialized US surround.

Cleaver's case amazes. A 1960s' Black Panther, reading the racial dilemmas all around him, sees a set of traps for heterosexuality. Is he homophobic? Decidedly so. But his homophobia is weirdly instructive.[7] Cleaver believes that "normal," heterosexual relations between Black men and Black women are plagued by their *loss* of sexual opposition. Black men and women are too much the same. (Recall my example of my friends from Harvard in chapter 1.) By virtue of their labor—largely manual, working-class, non-bourgeois in 1968, Cleaver claims—they are classed the same. And their *class* positions, Cleaver argues, are read by white culture as "founded in biology," since race keeps Blacks "down" in class.[8]

Blacks and whites were different sexes by dint of this "biology"? That's not exactly how Cleaver puts it, but the implication sits inside his words. By their class positions, Black men and women, according to Cleaver, are together gendered as strong-bodied, virile, lacking in sovereignty, split from their minds and drenched in their sex. (Is he contesting or *believing* these tropes? It's strangely hard to tell.) Cleaver is claiming that this shared positioning makes Black women and men the victims of sexual sameness. And so they pursue, as if they must, white men and women as their opposite sex.

Two things are telling. Cleaver believes, as if it were biological law, that only so-called opposites attract. Anything other than magnetic attraction between established opposites is homosexuality. Black on Black, for instance. That is to say, and this point startles, Cleaver reckons that, *by virtue of class*, Blacks are gendered masculine ("supermasculine" and "subfeminine") and whites are all effeminate. (Cleaver's is equal-opportunity offensiveness, as he maps the cultural myths of his day.)

Taken together, these factors make for an odd result. Fleeing sexual sameness leads to racial mixing. But this mixing looks "homosexual" (and also weirdly "hetero" at the same time!). See what you think, when Cleaver says:

> The [white man] is launched on a perpetual search for his alienated body, for affirmation of his unstable masculinity. . . . [He] cannot help but covertly, and perhaps in an extremely sublimated guise, envy the bodies and strength of the [Black] men beneath him—those furthest from the apex of administration . . . the men most alienated from the mind . . . (This is precisely the root, the fountainhead of the homosexuality that is perennially associated with [white moneyed men].)

Say what you will, but Cleaver's dated, homophobic thinking (soaking in its sexism) shows the incoherence of binary sex as a ground for heterosexual relations. People of the "same sex" (Black men and white men) can be *gendered* differently—*so very differently*—from each other that, as a pair of men, they can seem more of a hetero coupling than heteros can.

This is true of *Fight Club*, a film that grabbed the public in 1999 and grabs students still. *Fight Club* is riveting, even quite campy, because it can't tell its sameness from its difference—or maybe just its characters can't.[9] To put it briefly: the narrating man (played by Ed Norton as a corporate drone) is at first like a woman (who's named Marla), whom he despises, but you know he's going to love.

How are they alike? Both attend support groups for patients with cancer. Though they're faking cancer, both go there to cry—to be listened to by others—to escape the boredom and loneliness of life. What's wrong with modern life? Everything's a copy of a copy of a copy (there's your biggest sameness). Mass-produced consumer goods have us by the throat: everything's IKEA, Starbucks, the Gap. (We're each made "individuals" in the same way.)

The narrator comes to perceive this problem as a man's problem, a threat to men's manliness, even though the film is twinning him with Marla. Perhaps this sameness leads him, at last, to fashion his Fight Club, though he thinks a man who looks to be his opposite has developed it. This is Tyler Durden, played by Brad Pitt, who looks manly, ripped, and sexy—everything as a man the narrator is not. (Durden is an underclass maker of soap—squatting in a broken-down, "inner-city" house; rebel that he is, he's the furthest thing from a corporate drone.)

Do you smell attraction? *Fight Club*, for sure, is queer in many ways. To rediscover manliness, men put their bodies all over each other. They smoke post-coital cigarettes after fighting and move in with each other. Yet, even stranger, later we discover that what has seemed so "homo" throughout this film—the narrator's relationship with Tyler Durden (talk about a "bromance," talk about a "man crush")—is simply the narrator's projection of himself. He *is* Tyler Durden, but only in his mind. The Great Manly Man isn't on you, he is *in* you. You carry him in you as your ideal, even when, especially when, he's so different *from* you. Here you're heterosexual with yourself, which allows you escape from your girlfriend who is too much like you, according to *Fight Club*.

Fight Club's most compelling feature lies in its revealing something simple (and monumental): many men misrecognize what they're suffering *from*. They can't see they're hurting from effects of corporate wealth, *not from loss of manliness*. And what they suffer from, women suffer, too. (If you know *Fight Club*, you know it ends comically pursuing this point.)

This is the danger of binary thought. Dangers to many good things—our health, income distribution, fairness in labor, modes of well-being, relation to the land—result from masculine/feminine mandates that con us into thinking that devotion to these norms will deliver the good life that, in reality, corporate power and white supremacy reserve for themselves.

We can scout these dangers via racial histories. Each strikes a blow to "opposites attract." Each shows the harm of this fateful concept.

Racial histories: Each strikes a blow to "opposites attract." Each shows the harm of this fateful concept.

Labor and Land Undo Opposites

Take Toni Morrison. She denounced the chorus decrying Black men's feminization and the "devastating" outcome of the female-headed home.[10] These laments continued as Moynihan leftovers, and Morrison wasn't having it. She knew these genderings were prejudicial—how we supposedly know when Blacks have failed to make it. They don't conform to white-world opposites.

Morrison, by contrast, always mourned the reign of (straight) white gender: how it seduces Black people away from larger collectives, leading them into the tight, disappointing configuration of the couple. Thus if masculinity is defined as access to control of capital and control of women—especially in the family unit—Morrison doesn't lament its failures. She does depict in fiction Black men's puzzlement that genitals don't convey the privileges they promise. If there's a Black masculinity for Morrison, it has the structure of promise and letdown. Being promised something could seem masculine; getting let down could feel feminizing.

This is the broader story, however, of Black *unemployment* in the US. (As an Alabama leaflet puts it, during the Great Migration of Black people northward: "Are you happy with your pay? Would you like to go North where the laboring man shares the profits with the Boss? . . . Let's Go Back North. Where no trouble . . . exists, no strikes . . .

good wages, fair treatment. . . . Will send you where you can have all these things." In reality, in April 1919, after the Migration, the federal Division of Negro Economics conveyed that "99% of Chicago's black veterans were still unemployed, with little prospect of work in the immediate future."[11])

It's a dead end, Morrison warns, if we pay attention only to promise-and-letdown for men. Well-paid employment and circles of support for any Black person can answer "The Pain of Being Black," as she details in an interview of the same name given in 1989. And the female-headed home?

> I don't think a female running a house is a problem, a broken family. . . . Two people can't raise a child. . . . The notion that the head is the one who brings in the most money is a patriarchal notion, that a woman— and I have raised two children, alone—is somehow lesser than a male head. Or that I am incomplete without the male. That is not true. And the little nuclear family is a paradigm that just doesn't work. It doesn't work for white people or for black people. Why we are hanging onto it, I don't know. It isolates people into little units—people need a larger unit.[12]

Missing from Morrison, you might think, for all her sharpness, is a vital nod to specific threats to Black men—a lethal misandry—in the brutalities of law enforcement, homicide, and imprisonment. ("Homicide Is Leading Cause of Death of Black Males Age 44 and Younger," states a newspaper headline in June 2020.[13])

Now more than ever, after George Floyd's murder by the police, these threats glow in the public conscience. Whatever will finally be done about them, they don't make Black men and women "opposites" of each other—just at times distinct in how the law takes hold of them. (The #SayHerName campaign was an answer to the whiteness of the #MeToo movement and a way to highlight, with other lethal factors, the deaths of Black women at the hands of police. Breonna Taylor is a recent example, whose name is often spoken with Floyd's.) Black men and women are subject to *slow death* at similar rates (though poverty is higher for Black women), and *both* have died from HIV/AIDS at rates disproportionate to their percentage of the US population, though new diagnoses (as of 2018) were nearly triple for the category "black male-to-male sexual contact" compared to Black heterosexual women.[14] COVID-19 has hit Black folks, along with the Navajo Nation, the hardest in this country.

All kinds of remedies must be considered—especially how health care, alongside policing, must be reconfigured from the ground up to serve Black communities (along with other communities of color). But Morrison isn't wrong. Bounteous employment and a larger unit of communal support remain essential to redressing Black pain.

And labor and couplings and blocked collectives—met with murder by US law—are also central to other racialized US genderings. Other *sexes*, one might say.

The history of Asian immigration in this country illuminates these factors. If Cleaver thought all Black men and women were masculinized by their manual labors, the opposite is claimed for Asian immigrants to the US. They've been deemed feminized.

In her field-defining book *Immigrant Acts*, Lisa Lowe explains the most specific factor. Citizenship is the system producing the racialized gender of Asian (American) "men" and "women."[15] Were these sexes historically different from white and Black sexes in the US?

Certainly, different laws applied to them. Quite distinct laws governed how Asian men and women came into this country—compared to European populations coming here. And these laws distinguished *between* men and women of Asian descent. The Page Act of 1875 infamously stands in history as "the first restrictive federal immigration law" in the US.[16] More than that, it blocked the entry of immigrants considered "undesirable."

Who was officially not to be desired? Chinese women. That is, the law sponsored by Republican Representative Horace Page was designed to "end the danger of cheap

Chinese labor and immoral Chinese women." Chinese women at large were deemed prostitutes. They would threaten the moral, monogamous ways of white men— who, presumably, did desire them; otherwise no such law would be needed. And the American Medical Association believed that Chinese immigrants, especially women, "carried distinct germs to which they were immune, but from which whites would die if exposed." A murderous womanliness was ascribed to Chinese women, whose labors would kill men. Chinese men themselves were headed toward exclusion from legal status—in the Chinese Exclusion Act of 1882, which prohibited all Chinese laborers from immigrating—and toward their more intensified "feminization" if they stayed in US jobs.

How were they feminized? Already, before the Page Act, many Chinese men came to the US by themselves to work in the mines, on the railroads, and in the fields. And also in feminized forms of labor, then and later—"laundry, restaurants, and other service-sector jobs."[17] Due to the "relative absence" of Chinese wives to begin with, and later the out-and-out exclusion of Chinese women from the US, Chinese men lived in "bachelor" communities—excluded from the marital forms that supposedly made them men. After the Exclusion Act, a new crisis faced them: stay and be alone in the United States or return to China to "reunite" with wives, family, and children.

These exclusions, scholars state, "froze" the Chinese community in place for several decades—though there was the "Driving Out" in the 1880's with widespread violence in western states and massacres in Wyoming and Oregon. Not until 1943 was the Chinese Exclusion Act repealed—allowing for 105 Chinese people to enter each year—and not until 1965 were all legal barriers abolished.[18]

Many striking traces of this racial history live inside the "gendering" of Asian Americans, Lowe reminds us. In *Racial Castration: Managing Masculinity in Asian America*, David Eng offers a bold example that marks the Asian penis—as unsettling as this reduction sounds. A well-known play conveys this focus. It reveals that not just feminization sticks to Asian (American) men. A weird disavowal altogether of their genitals emerges, too.

The play is *M. Butterfly*, by David Henry Hwang, a sensation on Broadway in the late 1980s—based on a "real-life" story from the 1960s to the time of the play. At heart is the force of Western views of Asian *women*. Women born to serve. (Recall what we learned earlier from Lim about the Asian houseboy, similarly serving the colonial fantasies of hetero-and-homo Western men.)

At any rate, the straight, white, male protagonist of Hwang's play—a diplomat serving the French embassy in Beijing, China—Rene Gallimard—makes this speech: "There is a vision of the Orient that I have. Of slender women in chong sams and kimonos who . . . are born and raised to be the perfect women . . . It is a vision that has become my life."[19] This speech attends his suicide. Gallimard commits ritual death through seppuku, thus attempting to die with "honor" in order to sustain this colonial fantasy.

And his heterosexuality.

This French man had been having sexual relations with a diva he believed was female, not a Chinese man. (He didn't know that men played all the female roles in Beijing opera, given that women had been banned from the stage.) In a fateful moment the diva's penis is revealed to him—so Gallimard "knows" he was sleeping with a "man"—and Gallimard performs his suicide to straighten out his "mistake."

Performs is the word. Just before dying, Gallimard "don[s] the robes of the forsaken Japanese geisha Cio-Cio San"—from Puccini's 1904 *Madama Butterfly*—while he applies thick white makeup. Gallimard conducts his act in whiteface. Or, as Eng concludes: "Gallimard is forced to counter the disrobed diva with a transvesting act of his own. . . . Now that [the diva] is publicly the man, Gallimard must publicly become the woman." This preserves Gallimard's desperate "farce," which, despite its pretzel twists, rests on pedestrian colonial desires.

Opposites attract?

Your head might be spinning. But Eng would like you to consider the "refus[al] to see at the site of the Asian male body a penis that *is* there." Eng is not a Cleaver—not in the least. Quite a bit like Morrison, and right along with Lowe, Eng wants it known that those who "have bemoaned the predicaments of Asian American masculinity"— complaining that Chinese men, for instance, are depicted as "effeminate closet queens like Charlie Chan or . . . homosexual menaces like Fu Manchu"—tumble into traps of homophobic, sexist thinking based on their longing for conventional virility and the same old difference of Asian women.

A different set of traps caught Native Americans.

We've talked about the way that labor can undo sex/gender opposites and "opposites attract." Land, in addition, is no small factor. This matter is so massive it's hard to state in part. But if we consider, even briefly, the land grab "necessitating" Native peoples' genocide, we will sense the depth of this *sexual* atrocity.[20]

Just take the maxim "Kill the Indian, Save the Man."[21] This saying, which became widespread in its day, came from Richard Henry Pratt. Pratt had been a US Army officer who "educated" American Indian "prisoners" who had been captured while defending their homelands. Based on his experience, Pratt then founded the Carlisle Indian School in 1879. This was the first of the "Indian boarding schools," which took Native children from their parents, land, and customs to immerse them in American Christian culture and the *sexual stylings of white men and women*.

The maxim says it all: the Native man is not a man. He couldn't be part of opposites' attracting if he tried. The only hope for his sexual future and Native women's future was their being killed, in spirit and in culture. They would be *killed into being* "men" and "women." School would do the killing.

Something more astonishing, however, was happening: even this game was rigged from the start. Assimilation may have seemed on offer. That was the point of education, after all. But *failed assimilation* was nearly guaranteed (due to skin complexion and abusive school conditions that affected graduation rates) and was reinforced by what was taught in class. If you're being taught that everything "Indian" must be killed—or you're not a man—anything you "are" on the way to this (unachievable) result indicates your failure. Thus, if it weren't horrific enough to uproot people from their culture, land, and family, the practice of educative murder actually assured that a US man would *not* result, no matter what genitals Native people had. The failing of prospects for assimilation would be insurmountable. In many respects.

Skin color, obviously, was bound to doom "Indians" in the United States of the 1880s and for many decades (even to this day). "Blood quantum" rules, as they were known—the percentage of white ancestry, used to discriminate—went back to before the Thirteen Colonies. They were even *more* widely used after 1934, when the Indian Reorganization Act used blood quantum to determine distribution of federal monies, even for Native sales of land. This was the future failure-of-acceptance awaiting newly minted Carlisle graduates. Most *didn't* graduate. More than 10,000 children taken from 140 different tribes attended Carlisle from 1879 until 1918. Only 800 children ever graduated. (Another source says 158.) Double that number ran away. Corporal punishment and sexual abuse were extremely common.

All this was designed by the gentleman called "the Friend of the Indian," whose model school spawned twenty-six others, and who believed that Native children should abandon their tribal kinship patterns, convert to Christianity, and seek forms of labor among "the best classes" of (white) Americans. Clothing was key. Writes Luther Standing Bear:

> The civilizing process at Carlisle began with clothes. Whites believed the Indian children could not be civilized while wearing moccasins and blankets. Their hair was cut because in some mysterious way long hair stood in the path of our development. . . . High collar stiff-bosomed shirts and suspenders fully three inches in width were uncomfortable. White leather boots caused actual suffering.[22]

Girls wore dresses, as you might imagine.

And though these maneuvers looked like the "straightening" of American Indians, as Mark Rifkin so cannily asserts—an effort to "insert Indigenous peoples into Anglo-American conceptions of family, home, desire," and "identity"—one could take the logic just a bit further into its paradoxical aims.[23] Mary Zaborskis in "Sexual Orphanings" puts her finger on it. Native children were deemed strange and sinful (read: "queer") due to their Indigenous forms of kinship and sexuality. (These were also systems.) But these children, in being heterosexualized, were made *doubly queer* in being made into failed heterosexuals— failure awaiting them (always) in their "blood."[24] How did they fail to be heterosexuals? They could not be "men" and "women."

Exquisite new writings by Joshua Whitehead—an Ojibwe Cree, Two-Spirit storyteller and academic—show how these "gendercides" do not give rise to "the vanishing Indian" (a typical myth). Indigenous people are vitally shaping the here and now and future of lands, according to Whitehead, be they lands of earth or mind. Venture a literary spin with Whitehead and raucous, undeniable vitality will be yours.

His book of poems, *full-metal indigiqueer*, and his debut novel, *Jonny Appleseed*, are boisterous to their core, a riot of ideas. A sample description gives you a feel. The poems' main character, Zoa, is a trickster who "infects, invades,

and infests as a virus inside canonical and popular literature to re-center the lives of Two-Spirit individuals."[25]
Consider this infection a defense gone on offense, turning the tables on colonization, as Zoa "takes on the likes
of Shakespeare . . . Dickens, and Milton, romps through
the fields of cyberpunks and biopunks, takes notes from
popularized horror icons, and emulates contemporary
pop-culture phenomenons like Lana Del Rey, RuPaul's
Drag Race, X-Men, Grindr, and Peter Pan."

If you need a basket to hold this richness, Qwo-Li
Driskill, in *Asegi Stories: Cherokee Queer and Two-Spirit
Memory*, has you covered.

The basket, indeed, is hir reigning figure. Driskill
makes "weaving" the metaphor for *making* the past and
future of Two-Spirit life. The term Two-Spirit, as you may
know, is used by some Native people "to describe someone
whose gender exists outside of colonial logic."[26] Driskill
invites the echo of "queer." Indeed, Two-Spirit is broad *and*
specific (much like "queer" is). It's an "umbrella term," says
Driskill, that "references Indigenous traditions for people
who don't fit into rigid gender categories" and, simultaneously, may refer "to Native people who identify as Gay,
Lesbian, Bisexual, Transgender, and Queer."

What's getting woven for Two-Spirit people? Their
colonial past with "the Other stories" that ran against the
weave of colonizing forces. (These are what Maori scholar
Linda Tuhiwai Smith calls "dissent lines."[27]) Driskill dis-

sents from colonial histories told by the colonizers in their own time. Another sense arises. Driskill explains that a double-walled basket has two walls that share one rim. Hence, s/he will "doubleweave queer and Native," creating "a *third space* between the basket walls."[28] Driskill finds hir own space in this third space, as a (noncitizen) Cherokee *asegi aquandanto*: "'strange-hearted' person." (Note the tender caress of "strange.")

Where does Driskill go in *Asegi Stories*? Into the past as a gateway to the future. As Driskill puts it: "Gender binaries are central to the invasion and occupation of Indigenous land"; "resistance, then, must centralize gender and sexuality."

And "anomalies." It's the making-strange of categories—leading them to be less rigid—and the emergence of Cherokee values at critical junctures that impassions Driskill. "Anomalies," then, are "characters that dwell in liminal spaces and cross boundaries." Hence, the charm for Driskill in a traditional Cherokee story where borders are playfully crossed and cooperative labor (a Cherokee value) allows for a creative bio-intervention. This is the tale of "two little things hardly larger than field mice" who sought to join a game some birds were playing. When questioned by an eagle why they didn't join the animals with whom they belonged, "the little things" explained that their fellow animals had actually derided them and run them off "because they were so small." After group-consult, the birds decided "to make some wings for the little fellows," cleverly using "groundhog skin from the head of a drum." So, these little animals joined the birds.

There are also historical narratives of people deemed anomalous to colonizers' categories. A much fiercer space, then, for Two-Spirit story dwells in "the Queer Lady of Cofitachequi." She was not Cherokee. She was a female warrior whose body stood at the threshold of colonial invasions of Cherokee people. The scene is at a river, as Driskill tells it. The people of Cofitachequi, governed by a woman, see the army of Spanish conquistador Hernando de Soto just across the waterway. The year is 1540 in the land now known as South Carolina and de Soto's expedition is "the first mention in colonial records of Cherokee people." The Lady is a route to them. Why? De Soto needs her: needs her to guide him and needs her protection, along with her food, as he heads into Cherokee territory.

Colonial accounts of the Lady are conflicting. They can't fathom her, a female warrior. Here we greet a pattern in colonial interpretation. Cherokee people are "feminine (even in male bodies)" *if and when* they submit, as they "should," to colonial Spanish power; or they're "masculine (even in female bodies)" when they endanger "colonial desires." The Lady looks like she starts out one way—wanting to submit to de Soto and his men—then turns the other way—escaping from de Soto with a group of slaves.

More to the point, Cherokee systems are running through these stories. They remain unseen. Driskill wonders if "Cherokees' generosity"—what looks like the ladylike grace of the Lady—is mistakenly "seen as support of the Spanish rather than . . . expressions of a system of reciprocity or attempts at *duyuktv*." *Duyuktv* is "a system of balance and justice" "within all relationships with both the human and more than human world." (In Cherokee cosmology, the center of the spherical world is "mobile"— "like a spinning jack." Justice needs balance.) Driskill, too, thus employs conjecture concerning this story, since the written sources are colonial ones. S/he must work inside their cracks, finding hidden depths.

What is indisputable is that the later colonists sought to change Cherokee gender. We know what they wanted to change it *to*. Pre-invasion systems were matrilineal. Clan was central. "Women's brothers—not their husbands— were the central male figures to their children's lives"; women could remarry; short of having children with a clan member (this was taboo), they enjoyed "a great deal of sexual freedom." Township structures also gave them political influence. They presided over agriculture.

Post-invasion Cherokee life saw a range of impositions and internalizations of colonial gender. Sadly, no surprise. But there was something staggering. A colonial plan, shared by the likes of Thomas Jefferson in 1803. Here's how it went: stop the men from hunting; shift them to laboring (like women) in the fields; this will displace the women to their homes. What will this accomplish? Jefferson explains: "When they withdraw themselves to the culture of a small piece of land, they will perceive how useless to them are their extensive forests." One more thing: slaves would be needed to assist with intensified labor in the fields. "So along with plows and looms," Cherokees were urged to take on slaves. Not a small irony, since African slavery had "'actually been imposed on top of the . . . system of Indian slavery'" that had preceded it. These were layered systems.

Labor. Land. Enslavement. Straightening out "Indians" was a vast project. And no one, as we know, ever planned for their equality as "opposites" attracting. (The boarding schools are proof.) Driskill and Whitehead both thus speak of "re-beautifying" Native peoples' gender queerness for their own pleasures and their own plans.

Given this lineup of treacherous histories, many different histories—the piercing underside to "opposites attract"—the questions are at last: What new meanings can be worn on surfaces, be they genitals, cloth, or skin? How confront the layers of our (un)known depths?

ALLURING SURFACE, MYSTERIOUS DEPTH

Short take:
Surface is incredibly deep.

External genitals, skin color, clothes. These are surface matters and they mean the world to us—with a world of consequence.

Race is skin-deep and presses so dramatically on our minds and lives. Gender is likewise not just the story of system and word but also a tale of alluring surface and mysterious depth. How do I wish to dress, gesture, present, behave, in ways that are visible, perceivable to others? What can be gathered only as story that is conscious or unconscious, pooled behind my eyes, deep in my brain, hidden from others unless conveyed?

Are there depths to *systems*? What would this mean? What makes change? To gauge these tricky matters and

Surface is incredibly deep. External genitals, skin color, clothes. These are surface matters and they mean the world to us—with a world of consequence.

offer final questions, we must turn to underwear, skin, and tremors. Then, to racial reckoning. And, to end, a word.

Let us head to underwear by several different means.

Alluring Surface

Bring back to mind Billy Porter's Oscars dress.

A "tuxedo gown," he called it. An elegant tuxedo tapered to the waist where it flared voluminously into an ocean of fabric at the bottom. (To the Tonys he wore his "uterus dress"—deftly fashioned from a Broadway curtain—to support abortion rights.[1]) Accused of being "the singular cause of [the] emasculation" of Black men, Porter doubled down.[2] "It's a calling, it's a ministry, it's intentional. I know exactly what I'm here for. And that is power." Power to forge new gendered forms? Move whole systems? Inhabit a beauty off-limits to his sex?

Megan Rapinoe could say something similar. *GQ* says it. Wedding the soccer player's style to her push for women's equal pay, reporter Mari Uyehara writes: "And then she was there on the sideline: arms spread at full wingspan . . . faded pink lavender locks swooped back . . . chest puffed, back arched . . . Superman-style."[3] The pose would be dubbed "the Rapinoe" in time. And Rapinoe was the superman of soccer's "bad girls"—deemed so for their "excellence" and their particular "refrain of pay equity":

"'done just taking bullshit.'" "One dad told me," gushes Uye-hara, "that he wanted his sons to understand the Megan Rapinoe" proposition along these lines: "'It's not about . . . how big you are but how you can make a big impact . . . by your *aura*.'" Adds Uyehara: also by your glasses. (Rapinoe rocks her shades.)

Can innovations on the surface of a body change human systems and the depths of human minds? That's a heavy lift. Porter and Rapinoe are public stars. Both have money. Both have platforms. Neither is debilitated (that we know of). Both are changing gender's possibilities, but so are people we've never heard of. At the same time, systems roll on as so many people throw their bodies up against them.

This is the summer of Breonna Taylor and George Floyd and . . . hold this thought.

Taking Stock (Again)

No one really knows how genders are changing day by day. We can spot leaps—or shifts—as we look back. But we are riding the wave coming at us, which can be gleeful and cruel by turns.

We can innovate and fantasize. Organize. Push for system change. We can hope for herd immunity (safety in numbers for change-making persons). We can change from tragedy. We can minute by minute *fail* norms.

No one really knows
how genders are
changing day by day.
We can spot leaps—or
shifts—as we look
back. But we are riding
the wave coming at us,
which can be gleeful
and cruel by turns.

This failure isn't nothing. It can be painful—can cost you your life. It can be happy. Also ephemeral. Gender does change *because* we fail its orderings. Jacqueline Rose, writing at the time of Luce Irigaray, made this point: "The unconscious constantly reveals the 'failure' of identity. . . . [T]here is no . . . position for women (or for men) which is ever simply achieved. . . . 'Failure' is not a moment to be regretted. . . . Instead 'failure' is something endlessly repeated and relived moment by moment throughout our individual histories."[4]

Gender has been changing since it was invented. Gender's changeability isn't really new—but in *perceiving* it, people are advancing it, sometimes fighting it, and also undeniably accelerating it. Gender, let's remember, was invented in response to certain recognitions. Biology and medicine, after all, came to realize in their way that the binary of sex was imposed upon a range of human bodies and their lived desires. Some of these desires were for new-look surfaces, behaviors, and gestures.

We see surface changing. (So many genderqueer, trans, nonbinary, and even agendered people are crafting surface changes—Porter and Rapinoe are not at all alone—and figures like Lady Gaga have given their all to the cause of surface play.) Could there be new surfaces? At the same time, could we stop believing that familiar surface forms (a white male body or an Asian woman's surface) have predictable depths inside them? Orenstein's boys, after all, have a lot going on behind their eyes. If we were to reduce them to their privileged surface—those with white-boy surface—we wouldn't know that.

Privileged surface is enormously impactful. White skin, supremely. But also gendered surface that looks like a recognizable man or woman—according to the (un)spoken codes of one's day. People with these surfaces move with greater ease, potential power, far fewer stares, and the tag of "normal" attached to them. A word has even been coined for these surfaces that bespeak ease. The word is "cisgender." It's the seeming inverse—the normative flipside—to "transgender," in much the same way that "straight" is used in terms of "gay."

We need to ponder "cis." This little prefix means "on the same side as" (whereas "trans" means "across")—as if "cisgender" people have remained on the same side as their "sex assigned at birth." Two rich veins beg us to tap them. First, can we ever really know if we're on the side of our sex assigned at birth in *anything other than our surface looks*? (If I'm male-assigned and dress like a man, do I match my sex? Am I on its side? Do I have to be thinking and behaving like a man to side with "male" and "man"? Orenstein's boys are not behaving manly—in fact, they are cowering—when they side with each other as "men.") Second, is matching one's sex with one's clothes itself a simple business?

How do these dynamics mark cultural change?

We'll come back to "cis." Permit me to delve into clothes and skin as a way to get to it. Only then will we grasp how deep our surface goes.

Snapshot of Change: Surface of Cloth, Surface of Skin

No one contests the dramatic role of clothing in marking sex/gender.

Things have changed on this front, nonetheless. Men have become less afraid of their pants. That's one thing. The other is related. Now it's less certain the clothes you're seeing are rehearsing people's genitals. It used to be the case—largely the case—that our genitals were showing on the surface of our clothes—even on our heads in the form of our hair. Which is to say, most of us used to obey the suggestion (almost a law) that we wear gender-specific clothes, so that, with each other, we could read our genitals off of the wrappings designed to hide them.

What else explains our culture's investment in gender-differential clothes for men and women? Why, however, can women, if they choose, wear men's clothes to work or school, whereas men can't wear women's garments without drawing stares or even abuse? (And now some stares of love. Ask Billy Porter.) In fact, straight men—this is largely true for white men—might seem gay if they dress too well or give some conscious attention to their appearance. What can explain these familiar dynamics?

In a wacky claim, Freud imagines pubic hair as a natural model for human clothing, since it covers and conceals a woman's genitals. Here is the unconscious motive, Freud tells us, for women's contribution, their only contribution, to civilized development: plaiting and weaving, which in turn shows the vanity of women, which is women's shame. For the vanity of women, Freud famously informs us, is a "compensation for [their] . . . sexual inferiority."[5]

Vanity, in other words, is fancy-pants shame. Vanity's purpose, according to Freud, is the concealment of "genital deficiency." But this is no real concealment at all. Vanity is calling out, "Look at my cover!" By Freud's rendering, in spite of what he claims, clothing is not primarily concealment. It is not primarily a more attractive version of its model, pubic hair. Clothing, rather, is bold revelation, a cover turning inside out. It reveals the *category*, male or female, of the person's genitals it purports to cover.[6]

Or perhaps it used to, with greater regularity. Now you can't be sure. The groovy guy next to you, with his gorgeous beard, masculine chest, and cool men's clothes, may be the bearer (the very proud bearer) of genital lips. He may have lived decades under the cones of "girl" and "woman." And he might welcome being thought gay even when he isn't. Of course, it's now possible, increasingly probable, that a straight man looking his best will receive the tag of "gay" as a nod to his panache. That's a major change in the last two decades.

In fact, this development gives us a feel for how *advertising systems* meet *innovation* meet *herd immunity* in the realm of clothes.

Advertising, right along with clothing, conveys and produces gender. (Witness the Coke ad from 2018: "There's a Coke for he and she and her and me and them."[7]) Ads make change, even in retrograde, lumbering ways. There's the case of underwear. All through my childhood, underwear held the line for men: the line that divides straight from gay. So fragile were men assumed to be, so in need of a line that wouldn't smudge, that underwear ads for men didn't show *men* in their underwear. It was presumed that if men looked at men in boxers or briefs, they might get confused—might not know if they were desiring or identifying with the male image.

The first attempt at change was to use male models who were known athletes: a baseball pitcher in my own time, then Michael Jordan, then Joe Montana. If the model were an athlete, a man could look at him and know he was identifying (so it was supposed). Only with the rise of Calvin Klein ads in the 1990's would this change. Because gay culture was boldly coming out (partly due to AIDS), Calvin Klein ads, perceived as rather gay, were messing with the line that divides straight and gay: do you desire him or do you want to be him? (No one has worried that women in their underwear would confuse women.)

Fear was still evident around the millennium, according to Malcolm Gladwell's 1997 essay for the *New Yorker* "Listening to Khakis: What America's Most Popular Pants Tell Us about the Way Guys Think." Gladwell reminds us just how fraught clothes are for straight, (white) middle-class men. He doesn't mark race, but it's clear that men of color—particularly Black and Latinx men—have for a long time given themselves much greater latitude to dress with attention to style and dash. NBA players, going back to Walt Frazier of the New York Knicks, were often trendsetting in terms of men's clothes.

Be that as it may, Gladwell explores—in ways that sound funny—"the roundabout way" needed to sell white men their pants, since "the man in the middle [of the economic spectrum] . . . probably isn't comfortable buying clothes at all."[8] Taking a look at a Dockers campaign beginning in the fall of 1987, Gladwell examines "the notion of khakis as nonfashion-guy fashion," which "lure[s] men . . . with the promise of a uniform," "so as not to scare them." The point of these ads was "to talk about [fashion] in such a coded, cautious way that no man would ever think Dockers was suggesting that he wear khakis in order to look *pretty*," since if a man "knows he is attractive and is beautifully dressed—then he's not a man anymore. He's a fop. He's effeminate." He's deemed vain.

Take that in: men feel squeamish about men's pants.

Phenomena such as metrosexuality and the TV show *Queer Eye for the Straight Guy* (starting in 2003) have confirmed and changed these fears.[9] The label "metrosexual" showed a need to signal a new breed of straight men who liked clothing—their own clothes. The reality show known as *Queer Eye* (original installment) showed gay men—the Fabulous Five—refurbishing straight men, making them over, giving them permission to care about fashion—while, through it all, straight men could pose as helpless and hopeless about clothes and beauty, thereby *confirming* their obvious straightness.

Talk about a roundabout fantasy for straight men. The logic went like this: They don't turn to fashion, they are turned to it by others—queer men who eye them. Bearing no shame for their turn toward cloth and domestic sprucing up (which they seem quite sincerely to desire), they can truly say that they did not do it, would not have known how, may not know how to do it again. They are straight guys living the dream. A beautiful shame, which is not their own, has knocked on their door, walked right in and held them, as they have never been held, for the sake of their women, in other men's eyes.

Such were the contortions of some men's relations to their own clothes. More pyrotechnics have surrounded their relations to womanly clothes. In an article for the *New York Times*, published in the year *Queer Eye* arrived, a reporter told of being asked by the paper to wear, as an experiment, a tasteful Jean Paul Gaultier skirt "intended for men" on his daily rounds. "The neuroses quickly set in," wrote the journalist: "I went through a phase not unlike the stages of grieving."[10] "I called my wife, who helped by laughing uncontrollably." The reporter continued, "I was sure I could walk around East New York in the skirt without being beaten up. But no way could I hope to interview witnesses to a shoot-out and be taken seriously. . . . Out in the street I found myself trying to hide between telephone booths and cars. As people stared, it occurred to me that, when you are a guy in a skirt, pretty much any abuse that anyone heaps on you seems fair."

What a strange dynamic for straight sexuality. Loving, gentle men ask the women they love to wear the very garments that, in men's eyes, symbolize humiliation and invite abuse. For some straight men, the story ends here. For others, there has been a lessening of fear and a movement into pleasure surrounding clothes (and, at last, hair dye). Herd immunity has now been achieved for men who attend to their socks, shoes, watches, and form-fitting suits. Some young men have been playing with blouses and other forms of femininized clothing.[11] Largely, however, for men not trying to be gender nonconforming, genderqueer, or nonbinary, men's surface options have expanded only modestly, almost entirely inside "men's clothes." What comes next, we do not know.

All of which indicates Freud was weirdly right—about one thing. Not a small thing. Socio-political disadvantage has attached to women's clothes and caused psychic wounding for anyone not wanting to wear them.[12]

Then there is skin.

Cloth and skin touch each other. Cloth is worn on skin—also next to skin. They touch each other's meanings. Each is a surface that may be the object of prejudice, violence, attraction, and pleasure. Each may be physically marked with a wound (torn cloth, torn skin) and each can elicit psychic wounds because of the shame it is made to carry. Each can prompt pride and aesthetic glamor. That is, there is beauty.

Cloth and skin are different. Consider permanence. A person can far more easily remove her clothes than her skin, and can change kinds of clothes (from feminine to masculine, from glamorous to plain style). Skin is more fixed. Despite the role of lightening creams, used to lighten skin, let alone white people's frequent search for tans, most skin color is difficult to change. Then there's the complicated matter of choice. Civil rights activists, student radicals, critical race theorists, and many folks of color have lived the hate attaching to a racialized surface— any skin of color—Black skin most intensely—a surface that people *don't choose* for themselves.

Are clothes chosen?

Cloth and skin touch each other. Cloth is worn on skin—also next to skin. They touch each other's meanings. Each is a surface that may be the object of prejudice, violence, attraction, and pleasure.

To begin with, they are not. Parents choose our clothes in accordance with their wish to fortify our gender (or defy the fort). Beyond that point, it's not an easy question as to how young children, never mind adults, are choosing their clothes or running with the herd. It's a tougher question to assess how clothes affect us, often unconsciously, sometimes wildly consciously, forming us from the outside in. Certain cultural suggestions and imperatives—you must wear this, you can't wear that—have touched us to our core. If they didn't, there wouldn't be the story of clothing for men I've just told.

For many genderqueer, nonbinary, nonconforming, and transgender people, the question of "choosing" may feel loaded. The feeling goes beyond the pain of imposition (having clothes imposed). The clothes folks *long* for—the clothes they feel they *need*—they may view as sewn-to-the-bone cloth skins. Their defiance of norms can even lead to sacrifice, suffering, or murder—though murder due to clothing is mostly bound to skin: transgender women of color, quite specifically. (Their murder rate is frightening—and not abating.[13])

Cloth and skin, certainly, are each a vivid surface. Different, they remain. Indeed, I wouldn't know how to tell the story of skin I tell for clothes. What *has* changed? If Black skin is a trigger for police—look at that phrase— look at where we are in May 2020—how can one fathom the depths of Black surface in US minds?[14] They shall know you by your *surface*?

Surface is deep.

The Puzzle of "Cis"

Here's where things get complicated.

Tenderly, I grasp why "cis" has been coined. Instead of only trans folks always having to say who they are, why shouldn't non-trans folks be labeled, too? One can see the appeal of this move from a fairness standpoint. Cis people, please, declare *your* selves.

The problem with "cis" is the way it's often used. It drapes upon the whole of a person's gender. It *hasn't* been confined to referring to a *surface*. It hasn't quite allowed for mysterious depths—the *way* our surfaces press on our minds (consciously, unconsciously) and how these pressings are not so predictable and don't "express" a simple siding with our sex. Common definitions of "cis" sound like these: "Cisgender is a term for people whose gender identity matches the sex that they were assigned at birth." "The term cisgender is the opposite of the word transgender." "Cisgender relates specifically to gender rather than sexuality. A person can be cisgender . . . and have any sort of sexuality. For example, two men may be cisgender but one straight and one gay."

Tricky problems cling to these claims. There can be no "matching" of "gender" to "sex" if everyone's gender is in fact queer (as this book has argued). Is this presumption—that matching is possible—the ultimate self-delusion that has given sex/gender the death grip it's possessed? Trans/genderqueer/nonbinary folks have in different ways come to see that matching isn't possible. Straight men can't even match their pants (!). We have seen that *no one can live* the norms of gender that pretend to be ideal.

Moreover, the notion that "cis" marks gender, not sexuality, might deny the history of queer sexualities: how even masculine, straight-appearing gay men put their gender "normalness" hugely into question. What about nontransgender feminists? Are they "cis," though they have often dramatically questioned the content of the concepts "man" and "woman"? Aren't the contents of these concepts greatly changing (what is the content or identity of "man")?

To give one example of the tangle on hand: should a femme lesbian go by "cis" if her surface reads as conventionally feminine? Would such a label deny all kinds of invisible thoughts, modes of identifying and desiring, that might mismatch with the sex "female"? Who decides whether she is matching her sex in her mind, her private behaviors, her ideas?

"Surface" and "depth" are terms to explore. Do they help us? I believe we largely read from surface when we deem a person "cisgender." The phrase "cis-surface"—I haven't heard this phrase—I'm playing with ideas—*might* point solely to what a surface looks like, thereby *allowing for our not-knowingness* concerning what goes on in the depths behind one's eyes. Behind one's facade might be sloppy thoughtlessness concerning one's gender; or a rigorous struggle underway; or some strategy to give new contents to familiar surface. (After all, a person's surface factually doesn't tell us even of their genitals or sex assigned at birth, never mind their thoughts.)

The privilege of this surface is not to be forgotten as a factor in our lives. (Many couldn't forget if they tried.) Recognizable men- and women-surfaces do provide access and ease in many contexts (though at times danger for cis-surfaced women). Since you've surely noticed that I've not been talking race while talking "cisgender," there's another problem. Once we bring in skin—the color of one's skin—"cis" is multifactored. Or undone? How could your gender as a person of color match a (white) sex—that is, "male" or "female"—that has excluded you?

I have no answers. No one does, I think. But raising new questions gets at new potential for splitting what we see (if we're sighted people) from what we presume. The severing of surface-looks from hidden depths—even the hiddenness of our own depths—all the while looking for the possible bleed between alluring surface and mysterious depths—may hold some promise for word and system change.

Believe it or not, this is not where we end.

Trans Meets Disability

There are other surfaces, along with cloth and skin.

And they have systems and words attached to them. It might seem odd to describe disability as a surface matter. After all, folks who are "neuro-diverse" may have invisible cognitive challenges. Still, if they "out" themselves, they will wear a word, perhaps a set of words: *disabled*; *person with a disability*; *crip* (a word of defiance). In a moment, we'll see what happens when gender identity and disability intersect. "Gender dysphoria" will be on the table.

A memoir takes us there. Eli Clare's *Brilliant Imperfection* is the book, and his subtitle, "Grappling with Cure," states his nemesis. Diagnosis as a system, run by the system of the medical establishment, haunts every page. Cure, as medicine's steady obsession, is its sub-brutality. And there are words. *Mental retardation*, *cerebral palsy*, *schizophrenia*: these large cones were lowered on Clare. (*Retard* and *monkey* were supplied by other children.)

Clare begins his memoir with a simple sentence: "I am alive today because of medical technology."[15] The cause of his harm in so many ways—the medical world with its diagnostic systems—fosters his survival. "Otherwise, my mother and I would have been dead long before my first breath, dead as the ovarian cyst that grew beside me." Clare was born "no bigger than a grapefruit," "brain cells already dead and misfiring."

His surface marks him. At his surface, people read him. Or try to read him. "What's your defect?" people ask him. Then comes pity, praise, or prayers. But mostly comes the thought that he needs and wants repair. Money-raising charities—Goodwill, Easter Seals, the Salvation Army—raise money off of him (and people like him) to seek "a cure."

Clare doesn't want one. He would refuse one. "I have no idea who I'd be without my tremoring and tense muscles, slurring tongue." All these surface traits have formed his hidden "depths": what Clare thinks, believes, and cannot see. (We see words—or touch them via Braille—but we don't see thoughts, even our own thoughts. Words are surface forms. Thoughts are more mysterious: palpable but hidden.) Over time, Clare discovers how he wants to read his surface, how he *can* read his surface, applying different words, likening "my tremors to sunlight stuttering through wind-tossed trees, my slurs to an earthworm curling over itself, my stumbles to the erratic rhythm of a pileated woodpecker drumming a tree." In essence, "adaptation," Clare concludes, "carries far more appeal than treatment."

So does anger.

Clare conveys his rage over seeing Whoopi Goldberg, famous Black actress and comic, on a billboard. Sponsored by the Foundation for a Better Life, the billboard shows Goldberg, "head in hands, dreadlocks threaded through fingers," "furrow[ed] . . . forehead." The spare set of words on the billboard reads: "Overcaem dyslexia" (purposeful misspelling); "HARD WORK"; "Pass It On." Clare puts it this way:

> Let me turn [this] inside out. Maybe Goldberg became an actor exactly *because* of her dyslexia. Maybe she developed her kickass humor as a survival strategy to navigate the world as a Black, poor, disabled girl. . . . To pose individual hard work, rather than broad-based disability access, as the key to success for people with dyslexia is absurd and ableist. To pair a Black woman with the value of hard work in a country that . . . has, for centuries, exploited their back-breaking labor as maids and nannies, factory workers and field hands is demeaning and racist.

As I say, enraged. The words Clare offers to counter the billboard are "access, interdependence, community, and fierceness." (These chime with Morrison.)

There's a gentler side to Clare's appealing fury. Critiquing the documentary *Christopher Reeve: Hope in Motion*, Clare takes a pause to point to hidden depths. But, first, he's angry. Reeve played Superman in the 1970s, amid early versions of superhero films. After an accident (he fell off a horse), Reeve had quadriplegia and was on a ventilator. He became famous for his fighting spirit—the documentary "uses the words *overcome, fight, unwavering will, working tirelessly, amazing results*"—and Reeve himself declares: "There are some people who just don't really dare to hope."[16] Clare is maddened by these words. There are Reeve's entitlements (wealth, whiteness, an army of helpers) that aid Reeve's hope: entitlements not at all widely shared by others. And there are Reeve's relentless preparations for a cure, the very kind of focus that Clare finds distracting, judgmental, presumptuous. Still, Clare pauses.

The break Clare takes is to note how many privileged signs have flipped on Reeve, deep inside. (I hear Orenstein.) Clare takes a breather: "For a moment, I let go of my anger."[17] "I imagine his loss as deep as his drive for a cure." "Not far beneath his words, I hear the fear of body-mind change . . . and death."

The deeps are mysterious. They sit behind surface. How they make each other—surface and depth—through a back-and-forth unseen by ourselves—is also a mystery.

Certainly for Clare. Decades after birth, he wants a surface change:

> I thought I understood self-acceptance and love . . .
> until my gendered and sexed self started speaking.

When I listened, I discovered an unshakeable desire to reshape my body-mind using medical technology—first with chest reconstruction surgery and later with hormone replacement therapy.

He doesn't get himself: "Uncovering my desire to transition—to live as a genderqueer, a female-to-male transgender person, a white guy—challenged everything I thought I knew."

Clare lands smack-dab back in diagnosis. This is precisely where he doesn't want to be: where doctors have the power to say what gender "is," along with granting or denying access to their definitions. "During this time and place in history," Clare reminds us in 2017, "doctors have the authority to name and classify sex and gender, just as they do disability." Clare will have to gain "a letter of recommendation from a therapist" confirming Clare's diagnosis of "Gender Identity Disorder." His surgeon requires it. No letter, no surgery. No letter, no coverage. (He is like Obama's soldiers.)

Clare gets the letter. He submits to diagnosis, even though the diagnoses have been changing. (The *Diagnostic and Statistical Manual of Mental Disorders*—the *DSM*, as it is known—has gone from calling trans experiences "Sexual Deviations" to naming them, over time, "Transvestism," "Transvestic Fetishism," "Gender Identity Disorder," and now "Gender Dysphoria."[18]) And Clare feels queasy over seeking "plastic surgery," given its monetary structures of exclusion: "I thought about poor people who can't get the most basic of health care. During her pregnancy with me, my mother had no health insurance, received almost no prenatal care, and so the ovarian cyst that grew alongside me wasn't detected until the crisis of my birth." Where can Clare rest?

On the word "restoration."

Using the example of restoring prairie land, after the ravages of agribusiness use, Clare considers that one is not curing the land's prior damage. Nor is one returning the land to pristine times. Such are pipedreams. One is addressing the needs of the land—if it would thrive. The actions taken are multiple, uncertain, but determined. (Mow and burn the existing field; seek the mix of seed that will grow tallgrass; "stabilize" while "creating" soil.) Those undertaking these painstaking processes give their labor to the land (and each other). Beyond this "restoration," moreover, hangs a question: how does all this figure in "Land Back!" initiatives addressing stolen Indigenous land?

Clare is mindful of these matters, all the while implying that restoration isn't cure. There's no going back. The reality is as valid for people as for land: "Maybe the earth just holds layer upon layer of history."

There's wisdom to that line. Also recognition of the violence held in layers.

What Is Debility?

Implied in this book are layers of violence. There is the force of words imposed at birth. There is the fort (with all the inglorious associations of that term). There is clothing as a mandate, official and suggested. Meanings put on skin. Realms of diagnosis. So-called biology put on biology.

Racialized gender—that is, gender—exposes these layers. And there is *debility*. That's a little term with a horrifying spread.

This important word now stands for "the slow wearing down of populations"—"slow death," if you will—a life being snuffed in very slow motion—caused by the way state powers withdraw or withhold the resources that sustain life.[19] (Affordable health care, access to healthy, nutritious food, clean water, strong schools.) It is like a surgeon withholding a surgery—a life-confirming surgery—on the scale of communities and types of populations.

This slow death is shrouded from view, since its effects take place over time. It's not a disability. (No "accommodations" come with dying slowly.) You might not see it on the surface of a person. It might build beneath the skin.

We now see it.

COVID-19 has shown that many people of certain populations are far more susceptible to the spreading virus, given their battles with debilitating circumstances (slow death) on a daily basis. (Steady lack of health care, dearth of healthy food, environmental toxins . . .) The country now *knows*, can't unknow, that Black communities and Indigenous groups, alongside Latinx populations, are being hit disproportionately hard. COVID-19 is layering onto debilitating harms that were already there. Sadly, it took a virus to show it? To expose slow death?

We could answer with a question: it took a man's murder to expose a slate of murders? As with the virus, George Floyd's murder—so terribly spectacular—caught on camera—made deaths seen. Put a system on view. Those deaths were always happening, but now the debilitating arm of the law has become apparent.[20] To the extreme.

There are calls for *system* change from many different quarters. Black Lives Matter (BLM) activists are meeting with governors, mayors, congresspersons, who, just a month ago, considered them only dangerous extremists. By the time you read this book, you'll know what has happened . . .

And if you're now wondering, am I reading *Gender(s)*?—where has gender gone in this talk of debility?—I can swiftly gather what this book is saying. If we care to understand gender at all, we must fathom race in every aspect of its workings (fast death, slow death, debilitations targeted in racialized ways; also, joy).

Do we care to?

Just One Word

The fitting place to end is surely at the river, with the CRC. The Combahee River Collective's Black feminist lesbians prepared, after all, for BLM, which has its own exquisite intersections and its roots in "care."[21]

Care wasn't cant for the CRC. It wasn't sanctimonious talk. It wasn't tied to the ethic of care that women supposedly uniquely nurture in themselves and others. Care, as we saw in Combahee's Statement, came from reading the forces of debility aimed at them. They aimed back. Care was their word for system change. Nothing less would do.

Attentive to joy, labor justice, historical layers, and surface adaptations that meet with pleasure (think of Clare here—or Lil Nas X—even the lush Latina gestures rendered by Rodríguez), we will need plans to take us there. Many in the fields of gender studies, ethnic studies, and disability studies are organizing people across our institutions, alongside community scholars and student activists, to craft specific measures on the front of environmental antiracism. A recent piece in the *New York*

If we care to understand gender at all, we must fathom race in every aspect of its workings (fast death, slow death, debilitations targeted in racialized ways; also, joy).

Times displays this nexus: "Climate Change Tied to Pregnancy Risks, Affecting Black Mothers Most."[22]

Gender(s) has contested *sex* and *gender*—those two words that have dared to speak for us.

I would end with one.

"Care" holds the promise of exquisite speaking back, collective pushing back, creative giving back, all in the name of a fierce restoration that cannot go back in time.

Care to the fore, we head forward. There are plans between our lips.

ACKNOWLEDGMENTS

The gratitude I owe cannot be contained. Thinking shaped by life and lifelong conversations, alongside sometimes quiet contestations and public protests, permeates this book. People I've known for my whole existence—my loving parents and caring brother—and the chance encounters that get inside one's thoughts—have led to my perspectives. So has my scene of friendships, for life.

As has reading. How can I account for the words inside my head? The people I've cited and thanked for prior books remain so crucial. Here I'll add and underscore additions to my brain: Marlon Bailey, Ella Blanchard, Karma Chávez, Eli Clare, Kimberlé Crenshaw, Qwo-Li Driskill, Lisa Duggan, David Eng, Demita Frazier, Jules Gill-Peterson, Jack Halberstam, Terry Kogan, Eng-Beng Lim, Barbara Ransby, Juana María Rodríguez, Rebekah Sheldon, Barbara Smith, Beverly Smith, C. Riley Snorton, Joshua Whitehead, and Mary Zaborskis.

I'd be nowhere without the career-long influence on my work of Henry Abelove, James Baldwin, Kate Bornstein, Judith Butler, Anne Fausto-Sterling, Lisa Lowe, Toni Morrison, Sylvia Rivera, Eve Kosofsky Sedgwick, and Hortense Spillers.

Micki McElya and an anonymous reader (clearly expert on transgender) offered brilliant suggestions for strengthening the book's address to its range of readers. I couldn't be more grateful. And Victoria Hindley has been the superb editorial driver of this whole project, from invitation to indispensable intellectual conversation, crafting a model for editorial friendship of the highest caliber. Gabriela Bueno Gibbs has so warmly and beautifully assisted us. Also of MIT Press, Virginia Crossman has brought her formidable smarts to copyediting, for which I am full of appreciation.

As the dedication to this book makes clear, the School for Cultural and Social Transformation is where I think onsite. Four years old this summer of 2020, and comprising gender studies, ethnic studies, and disability studies, "Transform," as we call it, is served by the finest faculty, staff, and students imaginable. Since I read their writings and plot with them daily, they have carved my thoughts in ways I cannot fathom. I adore them, to a person.

Finally, I thank my chosen kin who read and commented on this manuscript—Becky Horn, Natalie Angle, Adam Weinstein, Lisa Duggan, and Shelley White—and my remarkable given family who just might read this book: Dave, Judy, Adam, Julie, Jon, Emily, and the person I affectionately call "Young Mare" (my cherished mother, Marilyn, who has survived my newly departed father, Edward). Shelley, of my heart, seems to grace my every line.

Agendered
This term now appears in *Lexico*, where it is defined as "denoting or relating to a person who does not identify themselves as having a particular gender."

Gender
This is the animating concept of this book. *Gender(s)* takes issue with standard definitions of the word *gender*. Still, it is helpful to know how the term has commonly been defined. According to *Merriam-Webster Dictionary*, gender is "the behavioral, cultural, or psychological traits typically associated with one sex." By contrast, contesting this binary view, *Gender(s)* argues that gender is strange, ungraspable, out of sync with "male" and "female," and weirdly not normal, since lived gender fails to conform to normative ideals and expectations, even when it is played quite straight.

Genderqueer
Wikipedia gives this explanation: "The term *genderqueer* originated in queer zines of the 1980s as a precursor to the term *non-binary*. In addition to being an umbrella term, *genderqueer* has been used as an adjective to refer to any people who are perceived to transcend or divert from traditional distinctions of gender, regardless of their self-defined gender identity."[1] Though I don't call all people "genderqueer"—I leave this term as a *self-designation*—I argue in this book that gender's queer for everyone.

Nonbinary
In its simplest sense, this term means, according to *Merriam-Webster Dictionary*, "not restricted to two things or parts." Therefore, *nonbinary* can refer to gender that is neither or both "man" and "woman"; or sex that is neither or both "male" and "female"; or sexual orientation that is neither or both "homosexuality" and "heterosexuality." *Gender(s)* persistently opens up problems with binary forms of any kind but confesses how hard it is to escape them, since they have so thoroughly structured lives and thought in US contexts.

Queer

Odd as it may seem, "queer" in this book doesn't specifically signify "LGBT" "identities," though they are included in queer. I mean queer in its broadest sense. I mean queer as "strange." Indeed, dictionaries offer this meaning for the word *queer*.

Racism

Encyclopedia Britannica gives a definition of this term that underscores matters of cultural belief (including belief in presumed biological underpinnings for race) and the role of systems: "the belief that humans may be divided into separate and exclusive biological entities called 'races'; that there is a causal link between inherited physical traits and traits of personality, intellect, morality, and other cultural and behavioral features; and that some races are innately superior to others." "The term," the *Encyclopedia* continues, "is also applied to political, economic, or legal institutions and systems that engage in or perpetuate discrimination on the basis of race or otherwise reinforce racial inequalities in wealth and income, education, health care, civil rights, and other areas." Ruth Wilson Gilmore gives this excellent, pointed definition: "Racism, specifically, is the state-sanctioned or extralegal production and exploitation of group-differentiated vulnerability to premature death."[2]

Sex

Alongside gender and sexual orientation, sex is one of this book's contested terms. Dictionary definitions tie sex to genitals or reproductive functions—that is, to biology. The twoness of sex also emerges. *Merriam-Webster Dictionary*, for example, defines sex this way: "either of the two major forms of individuals that occur in many species and that are distinguished respectively as female or male especially on the basis of their reproductive organs and structures." Look for how this book puts "sex" into question.

Sexism

Definitions given by *Merriam-Webster Dictionary* perhaps show the problem with sexing anyone, never mind babies who can't consent to the sex they're assigned. Here are that dictionary's two definitions: "prejudice or discrimination based on sex; *especially*: discrimination against women"; "behavior, conditions, or attitudes that foster stereotypes of social roles based on sex." *Gender(s)* is asking if the assignment of sex from birth doesn't already presume behaviors, conditions, or attitudes that will make the sexes distinct. If not, why insist on sexing babies? Why the investment in the distinction?

Transgender

"Trans" has sometimes meant the movement from one fixed pole of sex and gender to another. For example, these wordings are sometimes used by transgender people: "assigned male at birth" to "woman" or "assigned female at birth" to "man." Now, more commonly, "transgender" (also) names those who do not feel right in their sex assigned at birth.

NOTES

Introduction

1. We learn of this Arizona catastrophe inside a CNN report on a gender-reveal party gone wrong in Australia: Emily Dixon, "Australian Gender Reveal Party Goes Wrong as Car Bursts into Flames," CNN, July 9, 2019, https://cnnphilippines.com/world/2019/7/9/gender-reveal-car-in-flames-Australia.html?jfdshfs.

2. Quoted in Lourdes Garcia Navarro, "Woman Who Popularized Gender-Reveal Parties Says Her Views on Gender Have Changed," All Things Considered, NPR, July 28, 2019, https://www.kunc.org/post/woman-who-popularized-gender-reveal-parties-says-her-views-gender-have-changed#stream/0.

3. Sage Lazzaro, "Tinder Just Became Trans and Non-Conforming Inclusive with 37 New Gender Options," *Observer*, November 15, 2016, https://observer.com/2016/11/tinder-just-became-trans-and-non-conforming-inclusive-with-37-new-gender-options/.

4. See, for example, Farhad Manjoo, "It's Time for 'They,'" *New York Times*, July 10, 2019, https://www.nytimes.com/2019/07/10/opinion/pronoun-they-gender.html.

5. Quoted in Shea Simmons, "Billy Porter's 2019 Oscars Gown Gave Him Power He Didn't Know He Had," *Bustle*, January 9, 2020, https://www.bustle.com/p/billy-porters-2019-oscars-tuxedo-gown-gave-him-power-he-didnt-know-he-had-19780882.

6. For definitions of these terms, see: "sex (*n.*)," *Merriam-Webster*, accessed December 1, 2020, https://www.merriam-webster.com/dictionary/sex#:~:text=b%20%3A%20sexual%20intercourse,sexed%3B%20sexing%3B%20sexes; and "gender (*n.*)," *Merriam-Webster*, accessed December 1, 2020, https://www.merriam-webster.com/dictionary/gender.

7. For spread inside and around "transgender" (and much more), see Jack Halberstam, *Trans*: A Quick and Quirky Account of Gender Variability* (Oakland: University of California Press, 2018).

8. Marxist terms for class—*bourgeois, petit bourgeois, proletariat, lumpenproletariat*—can be useful, in numerous contexts, but the complicated realms of white collar, pink collar, pink proletariat, and corporate drone (to name just a few) show the many different scenes of labor emergent since the nineteenth-century context of Marx (no surprise). Even the popularization,

not long ago, of "the 1 percent vs. the 99 percent" is telling of the US context.

9. Kathryn Bond Stockton, *Making Out* (New York: New York University Press, 2019).

10. Eliana Dockterman, "A Doll for Everyone," in "The Science of Gender," special issue, *Time* (New York: Meredith Corporation, 2020): 88.

11. "Creatable World™," Mattel, accessed September 22, 2020, https://www.mattel.com/en-us/creatable-world.

12. Dockterman, "A Doll for Everyone," 90. Other quotations from this section are from pages 90, 91, 92, 91.

13. Robin Bernstein, *Racial Innocence: Performing American Childhood from Slavery to Civil Rights* (New York: New York University Press, 2011), 69, 71. Bernstein also provides her own intriguing take on (what became known as) the Clarks' Doll Tests that were cited in *Brown v. Board of Education* (1954)—the landmark Supreme Court case that desegregated US public schools. See Bernstein, 235–243. For an explanation of the doll tests, see: https://www.naacpldf.org/ldf-celebrates-60th-anniversary-brown-v-board-education/significance-doll-test/.

14. Tracy E. Gilchrist, "One Million Moms: Mattel's Gender-Inclusive Dolls Promote 'Sin,'" *ADVOCATE*, October 2, 2019, https://www.advocate.com/business/2019/10/02/one-millions-moms-mattels-gender-inclusive-dolls-promote-sin.

15. Quoted in Julie Moreau, "Year after Trans Military Ban, Legal Battle Rages On," OUT Politics and Policy, NBC News, April 11, 2020, https://www.nbcnews.com/feature/nbc-out/year-after-trans-military-ban-legal-battle-rages-n1181906.

16. For this definition, see: "gender dysphoria (*n.*)," *Lexico*, accessed December 1, 2020, https://www.lexico.com/definition/gender_dysphoria.

17. Donald J. Trump (@realDonald Trump), "After consultation with my Generals and military experts," Twitter, July 26, 2017, 8:55 a.m., 9:04 a.m., 9:08 a.m., https://twitter.com/realDonaldTrump/status/890193981585444864.

18. For example, see Alex Horton, "'The Military's #MeToo': Vanessa Guillén's Slaying Has Many Servicewomen Revisiting Their Own Deep Scars," *Washington Post*, July 7, 2020, https://www.washingtonpost.com/national-security/2020/07/07/vanessa-guillen-servicewomen-veterans/.

19. Michel Foucault, *Discipline and Punish: The Birth of the Prison*, trans. Alan Sheridan (New York: Vintage, 1979), 164.

20. Jonathan Martin, dir., *World War I in Color* (Silver Spring, MD: Acorn Media, 2010), DVD.

21. I have explored this issue at length in Kathryn Bond Stockton, "Cloth Wounds," in *Beautiful Bottom, Beautiful Shame: Where "Black" Meets "Queer"* (Durham, NC: Duke University Press, 2006), 39–66.

22. Claire Friedman, "The Electable Female Candidate," *New Yorker,* December 16, 2019, 29.

23. Here is a link showing this policy change from September 4, 2014 (since taken down from Mount Holyoke's own website): https://www.campuspride .org/mount-holyoke-becomes-second-all-womens-college-to-formally-invite -transgender-applicants/.

24. "Mission and Gender Policy," Wellesley College, accessed September 23, 2020, https://www.wellesley.edu/news/gender-policy.

25. For this definition, see: "Latinx (*n.*)," Google, accessed December 1, 2020, https://www.google.com/search?q=definition+of+latinx&oq=definition+of+ Latinx&aqs=chrome.0.0i457.5625j1j7&sourceid=chrome&ie=UTF-8.

26. Claudia Milian, *LatinX* (Minneapolis: University of Minnesota Press, 2020), 9. Subsequent quotations in this section are from pages 19, 10, 15, 15, 15, 15, 11, 27.

27. Terry Moore, "Why Is 'X' the Unknown?," TED Talk, February 2012, https:// www.ted.com/talks/terry_moore_why_is_x_the_unknown?language=en.

28. Andrew R. Chow, "Old Town, New Road: How 20-Year-Old Upstart Lil Nas X Used the Internet to Beat Nashville at Its Own Game," *Time,* August 26, 2019, 56. The next two quotations in my text are also from this page.

29. nope (@LilNasX), "wow man last year i was sleeping on my sisters floor," Twitter, July 28, 2019, 1:40 p.m., https://twitter.com/LilNasX/status /1155533398351458304.

Chapter 1

1. For a fascinating index of this matter, see Alice Randall, *The Wind Done Gone* (New York: Mariner, 2002), a literary parody of *Gone With the Wind*.

2. On the fear of child sexuality, see Kathryn Bond Stockton, *The Queer Child, or Growing Sideways in the Twentieth Century* (Durham, NC: Duke University Press, 2009) and Steven Angelides, *The Fear of Child Sexuality: Young People, Sex, and Agency* (Chicago: University of Chicago Press, 2019).

3. Anne Fausto-Sterling, *Sex/Gender: Biology in a Social World* (New York: Routledge, 2012), 4. Subsequent quotations in my text are from pages 4, 3, 4, 4, 4, 4; emphasis in quotes from page 4 is in the original.

4. See Katrina Karkazis, *Fixing Sex: Intersex, Medical Authority, and Lived Experience* (Durham, NC: Duke University Press, 2008).

5. Fausto-Sterling, *Sex/Gender*, 4. Subsequent quotations in my text are from pages 4, 6, 10.

6. Avgi Saketopolou, "Risking Sexuality Beyond Consent: Overwhelm and the Suffering of Pleasure in Jeremy O. Harris's *Slave Play*" (unpublished manuscript, consulted on July 12, 2020), 6.

7. Fausto-Sterling, *Sex/Gender*, 27. Subsequent quotations from Fausto-Sterling are from pages 32, 44, 30, 33, 33.

8. Quoted in Markham Heid, "Biology and the Brain," in "The Science of Gender," special issue, *Time* (New York: Meredith Corporation, 2020), 14.

9. Quoted in Jeffrey Kluger, "Not That Different from One Another," in "The Science of Gender," special issue, *Time* (New York: Meredith Corporation, 2020), 15.

10. Fausto-Sterling, *Sex/Gender*, 34. The subsequent quotations from Fausto-Sterling are from page 37.

11. Andrew Sullivan, "The He Hormone," *New York Times Magazine,* April 2, 2000, 1. For online access, see: https://www.nytimes.com/2000/04/02/magazine/the-he-hormone.html. Subsequent quotations in my text are from pages 1, 3, 2, 2, 3, 3, 5, 5, 5, 2, 1–2, 3.

12. This great phrase is from Rebecca M. Jordan-Young and Katrina Karkazis, *Testosterone: An Unauthorized Biography* (Cambridge, MA: Harvard University Press, 2019), 1.

13. Sullivan, "He Hormone," 4. Subsequent quotations from Sullivan in this section are from pages 4, 4, 4, 2, 6, 7, 8, 8, 8, 14, 14, 15, 15, 15, 15.

14. The clitoris can get larger via testosterone injections, but it does not become a penis.

15. On the matter of attraction, see, for example, Zhana Vrangalova, "Research Shows Many Trans Folks' Sexual Attractions Change after Transition," *them.*, June 25, 2018, https://www.them.us/story/sexual-attraction-after-transition. The subheading to this piece refers specifically to a trans man: "Toby was exclusively attracted to women before he transitioned. Now he's attracted to men, too." As for phalloplasty among trans men, one should take percentages with a grain of salt, given that the definitions of "trans" are currently fluid and many trans-identified people are not "out" to others. With these major caveats, see, for example, Ian T. Nolan, Christopher J. Kuhner, and Geolani W. Dy, "Demographic and Temporal Trends in Transgender Identities and Gender Confirming Surgery," *Translational Andrology and Urology* 8, no. 3 (June 2019): 184–190.

16. See my chapter "Bottom Values," in Stockton, *Beautiful Bottom, Beautiful Shame*.

17. Daniel Geary, "The Moynihan Report: An Annotated Edition," *Atlantic*, September 14, 2015, https://www.theatlantic.com/politics/archive/2015/09/the-moynihan-report-an-annotated-edition/404632/.

18. Evan Urquhart, "The Lie Hormone," *Slate,* January 22, 2018, https://slate.com/human-interest/2018/01/andrew-sullivans-ode-to-testosterone-is-rooted-is-stereotypes.html, 3. Subsequent quotations in my text are from pages 3, 3, 3, 2.

19. Jordan-Young and Karkazis, *Testosterone*, 4–5. Subsequent quotations are from pages 6, 7, 7, 9, 5, 5, 5, 5, 6, 6, 15.

20. See Jordan-Young and Karkazis, *Testosterone*, 70–76. In a section entitled "Honor Cultures: To Be Young, Violent, and Black," the authors show how "the most frequently cited article in the scientific literature on dominance, aggression, or violence and T among humans"—a think piece by Allan Mazur and Alan Booth—"has the feel of an empirical study" but is full of "simple speculations, stitched together by familiar stories about race," presenting "no data on violence or crime among black men, nor on the stresses that black men face."

21. Peggy Orenstein, *Boys & Sex* (New York: Harper Collins, 2020). Her website (https://www.peggyorenstein.com/boysandsex) includes this testimonial from Nick Kroll, co-creator, writer, and star of *Big Mouth*.

22. Peggy Orenstein, "The Miseducation of the American Boy: Why Boys Crack Up at Rape 'Jokes,' Think Having a Girlfriend Is 'Gay,' and Still Can't Cry—and Why We Need to Give Them New and Better Models of Masculinity," *Atlantic,* January/February 2020, 65. Subsequent quotations in my text are from pages 65, 65, 64, 64, 64, 64, 65.

23. The George W. Bush "preemptive strikes" doctrine was "a defense against an immediate or perceived future threat to the security of the United States." "Bush Doctrine," Wikipedia, accessed December 1, 2020, https://en.wikipedia.org/wiki/Bush_Doctrine#:~:text=It%20was%20used%20to%20describe,security%20of%20the%20United%20States.&text=Generally%2C%20the%20Bush%20Doctrine%20was,unilaterally%20pursue%20U.S.%20military%20interests. With regard to the police, see David Brooks, "The Culture of Policing Is Broken," *Atlantic,* June 16, 2020, https://www.theatlantic.com/ideas/archive/2020/06/how-police-brutality-gets-made/613030/, where he writes: "Then there is the constant presence of unacknowledged fear. As Seth Stoughton, a University of South Carolina law professor, wrote in *The Atlantic* in 2014, police officers 'shoot because they are afraid. And they are afraid because they are constantly barraged with the message that they should be afraid, that their survival depends on it.'"

24. Orenstein, "The Miseducation of the American Boy," 65. The next two quotations are from pages 66 and 68, respectively.

25. Peggy Orenstein, "Peggy Orenstein on 'Boys & Sex,'" interview by Doug Fabrizio, Radiowest, January 24, 2020, https://radiowest.kuer.org/post/peggy-orenstein-boys-sex.

26. Orenstein, "The Miseducation of the American Boy," 68. Subsequent quotations are from pages 68, 68, 68, 68, 69–70, 69–71, 71, 71, 72.

27. Stephanie Harzewski, *Chick Lit and Postfeminism* (Charlottesville: University of Virginia Press, 2011), 22. Subsequent quotations in my text are from pages 194, 23, 23, 3, 98, 195, 8, 33, 33, 33, 36, 10, 10, 57, 57, 168, 149, 150, 155.

28. "Colorblind" is offensive on two different fronts: for its racist underpinnings and its ableist assumptions. I use it here because it has (sadly) been so baked into the cake of US political discourse on race.

29. Gay bars, in earlier times (and still), have functioned as social closets for a range of queer-identified people.

30. For a 2019 interview with Marlon Bailey and Rashaad Newsome, see: Meghna Chakrabarti and Anna Bauman, "The Growth (and New Contexts) of LGBTQ Ball Culture," WBUR, December 11, 2019, https://www.wbur.org/onpoint/2019/12/11/ballroom-scene-lgbtq-ball-culture-vogue.

31. Marlon M. Bailey, *Butch Queens Up in Pumps: Gender, Performance, and Ballroom Culture in Detroit* (Ann Arbor: University of Michigan Press, 2013), 8. The quotations in this section are from pages 16, 17, 36, 48, 60, 58, 58, 59, 58.

32. The remarkable Dorian Corey in *Paris Is Burning* (directed by Jennie Livingston, 1990) made this point in her inimitable way.

33. Bailey, *Butch Queens*, 65. Subsequent quotations in my text are from pages 65, 66, 66.

34. Juana María Rodríguez, *Sexual Futures, Queer Gestures, and Other Latina Longings* (New York: New York University Press, 2014), 2. Subsequent quotations in my text are from pages 2, 2, 2, 2, 2, 2, 2, 2, 2, 3, 5, 5, 148, 149, 149, 151, 154, 158, 180.

35. Rodríguez tells us this show was presented in 2007 in Seattle, Washington, "as part of *Kaleidoscope: National People of Color Cabaret*" (148).

36. Rodríguez writes: "The National Prison Project of the ACLU, using only the documents available to it through the Freedom of Information Act, found over two hundred *reported* cases of sexual abuse in detention facilities between 2007 and 2011." You can visit their current website at: https://www.aclu.org/issues/immigrants-rights/immigrants-rights-and-detention/sexual-abuse-immigration-detention-0.

37. Eng-Beng Lim, *Brown Boys and Rice Queens: Spellbinding Performance in the Asias* (New York: New York University Press, 2014), ix. Subsequent quotations in my text are from pages 1–2, 2, 2–3, 3, 3, 5–6, 6, 10, 42, 17, 43, 17, 46.

Chapter 2

1. This definition comes from the Intersex Society of America: "What Is Intersex?," accessed December 1, 2020, https://isna.org/faq/what_is_intersex/.

2. Is Gill-Peterson imposing a current category—transgender, specifically—on children from an earlier time? Indeed, she is using "trans" in its broad sense, "as it has been theorized in transgender studies, sometimes as a prefix and sometimes with an asterisk, to mark a *political* distinction from medical or pathological meanings that have accrued to the term 'transgender' in recent years, many of which have been borrowed from the earlier term 'transsexual'" (*Histories of the Transgender Child* [Minneapolis: University of Minnesota Press, 2018], 8). Is her use of "trans" for a child in the 1930s "technically anachronistic"? Yes, she says. But "I do so precisely to make an intervention." It's one also made by transgender scholar Susan Stryker: "to [tell] a story about the political history of gender variance that is not limited to one experience"—here, a current trans child narrative that has earlier and different roots (8). Gill-Peterson points to my concept of the "ghostly gay child" in the twentieth century as a cognate concept (9–10). (See Stockton, *The Queer Child*, 17–22.)

3. Gill-Peterson, *Histories of the Transgender Child*, 3. Subsequent quotations in my text are from pages 4, 79, 26–27, 119, 119, 119.

4. Gayle Rubin, "The Traffic in Women: Notes on the 'Political Economy' of Sex," in *The Second Wave: A Reader in Feminist Theory*, ed. Linda Nicholson (New York: Routledge, 1997), 28. Subsequent quotations from Rubin in this section are from pages 28, 28, 29, 33, 36.

5. For a great book on the complicated permutations of the concept "single," see Michael Cobb, *Single: Arguments for the Uncoupled* (New York: New York University Press, 2012).

6. Rubin, "Traffic," 37. Subsequent quotations are from pages 37, 39, 39, 40, 40.

7. See *Near the Big Chakra* (1971), "Plot Summary," accessed October 5, 2020, https://www.imdb.com/title/tt0158020/plotsummary?ref_=tt_ov_pl.

8. In French, the word *sexe* is used to mean biological category, genitals, and sexuality—a trifecta of conflation.

9. Luce Irigaray, *This Sex Which Is Not One*, trans. Catherine Porter with Carolyn Burke (Ithaca, NY: Cornell University Press, 1985), 23.

10. My last phrase here—"how preserve its pleasures"—is critical because the "plasticity" of children's bodies, as Gill-Peterson has so schooled us, led to the medical terrors rained upon them.

11. Irigaray, *This Sex*, 31. The subsequent quotation in my text is from page 174.

12. For the contemporary context that birthed the Black Lives Matter Movement (more officially known as the Movement for Black Lives), see the excellent study by Barbara Ransby, *Making All Black Lives Matter* (Berkeley: University of California Press, 2018).

13. For online access to the Statement, go to: https://www.blackpast.org /african-american-history/combahee-river-collective-statement-1977/.

14. For this definition, see: "confluence (*n*.)," Google, accessed December 2, 2020, https://www.google.com/search?q=definition+of+confluence&oq=defi nition+of+confluence&aqs=chrome..69i57j0l2j0i22i30l5.11476j1j7&sourceid =chrome&ie=UTF-8.

15. Barbara Smith uses this phrase from Frazier for the title of Smith's essay, "Doing It from Scratch: The Challenge of Black Lesbian Organizing," in *The Truth that Never Hurts: Writings on Race, Gender and Freedom*, ed. Barbara Smith (New Brunswick, NJ: Rutgers University Press, 1998), 171–172. The next quotation in my text is also from Smith's essay, page 172.

16. Keeanga-Yamahtta Taylor, ed., *How We Get Free: Black Feminism and the Combahee River Collective* (Chicago: Haymarket Books, 2017), 17. Subsequent quotations in my text are from pages 17, 6, 18, 20, 20, 19, 20.

17. Barbara Smith, "Racism and Women's Studies," in *Intersectionality: Foundations and Frontiers*, 2nd ed., ed. Patrick R. Grzanka (New York: Routledge, 2019), 64. The subsequent quotations in my text are from page 64.

18. Kimberlé Williams Crenshaw, "Demarginalizing the Intersection of Race and Sex: A Black Feminist Critique of Antidiscrimination Doctrine, Feminist Theory, and Antiracist Politics," *Chicago Legal Forum* (1989): 139–168.

19. Kimberlé Williams Crenshaw, "The Structural and Political Dimensions of Intersectional Oppression," in *Intersectionality: Foundations and Frontiers*, 2nd ed., ed. Patrick R. Grzanka (New York: Routledge, 2019), 43.

20. Quoted in Patrick R. Grzanka, "Intersectional Objectivity: On Knowledge and Violence," in *Intersectionality: Foundations and Frontiers*, 2nd ed., ed. Patrick R. Grzanka (New York: Routledge, 2019), 6.

21. For example, see Patricia Hill Collins, *Black Feminist Thought: Knowledge, Consciousness and the Politics of Empowerment* (London: Hyman, 1990) and Beverly Guy-Sheftall, ed., *Words of Fire: An Anthology of African-American Feminist Thought* (New York: Norton, 1995).

22. Shuddhabrata Sengupta, "Identity as a Weapon of Mass Destruction," in *Intersectionality: Foundations and Frontiers*, 2nd ed., ed. Patrick R. Grzanka (New York: Routledge, 2019), 121. Subsequent quotations in my text are from page 119.

23. Marie-Claire Belleau, "L'intersectionalité: Feminisms in a Divided World," in *Feminist Politics: Identity, Difference, Agency*, ed. Deborah Orr et. al. (Lanham, MD: Rowman & Littlefield, 2007), 51–62. For a different term, "switchpoint," that I have theorized, see Stockton, *Beautiful Bottom*, 4–5.

24. Karma R. Chávez, *Queer Migration Politics: Activist Rhetoric and Coalitional Possibilities* (Urbana: University of Illinois Press, 2013), 80. Subsequent quotations in my text are from pages 79, 81, 81, 80, 110, 110, 110, 110, 110.

25. Jesus Cisneros, "Undocuqueer: Beyond the Shadows and the Closet," in *Intersectionality: Foundations and Frontiers*, 2nd ed., ed. Patrick R. Grzanka (New York: Routledge, 2019), 324. Subsequent quotations in my text are from pages 325, 326, 328.

26. Chávez, *Queer Migration*, 111.

27. Cherríe Moraga, *Loving in the War Years: Lo que nunca pasó por sus labios* (Cambridge, MA: South End Press, 2000), iii. Subsequent quotations in my text are from pages iii, iii, 110, 50, 8, 52, 44, 52, 82.

28. Hortense J. Spillers, "Mama's Baby, Papa's Maybe: An American Grammar Book," *Diacritics* (Summer 1987): 72. The subsequent quotations from Spillers in my text are also from page 72.

29. C. Riley Snorton, *Black on Both Sides: A Racial History of Trans Identity* (Minneapolis: University of Minnesota Press, 2017), 17. Subsequent quotations in my text are from pages 20, 20, 53, 25, 19, 27, 24.

Chapter 3

1. Plato, *The Symposium*, trans. Walter Hamilton (New York: Penguin, 1951), 192c.

2. Stockton, *Making Out*, 90–91.

3. HB 2, General Assembly of North Carolina, Second Extra Session 2016, Session Law 2016-3, House Bill 2, Part I, S 115C-521.2, (b), https://www.ncleg.net/sessions/2015e2/bills/house/pdf/h2v4.pdf.

4. See Mihir Zaveri, "Virginia Schools' Bathroom Rule Violates Transgender Rights, U.S. Judge Says," *New York Times*, August 9, 2019, https://www.nytimes.com/2019/08/09/us/virginia-transgender-bathroom-policy.html.

5. Terry Kogan, "Sex-Separated Restrooms: An Exploration in Architecture, Gender & Law" (unpublished manuscript, consulted on June 16, 2020), 2. Subsequent quotations in my text are from pages 2, 4, 4, 4, 4, 5, 8, 9. This

manuscript draws on Kogan's numerous published essays on this subject. For more on the *Stalled!* Project, see https://www.stalled.online/.

6. Geary, "The Moynihan Report."

7. See my chapter "Erotic Corpse" on Eldridge Cleaver, Emmett Till, and James Baldwin in Stockton, *Beautiful Bottom*, 149–176. My chapter doesn't scrimp on Cleaver's madcap, frightening contradictions, on and off the page.

8. Eldridge Cleaver, *Soul on Ice* (New York: Dell, 1968), 189. The subsequent quotation from Cleaver is from page 182.

9. David Fincher, dir., *Fight Club* (Los Angeles: 20th Century Fox, 1999).

10. For one index of this matter, see the cover story "Black and White in America," *Newsweek*, March 7, 1988, 20, https://www.ebay.com/itm/NEWSWEEK-Magazine-March-7-1988-Black-White-Integrated-America-Winter-Olympics-/333683344949.

11. Philip S. Foner, *Organized Labor and the Black Worker, 1619–1981*, 2nd ed. (New York: International Publishers, 1982), 130, 132.

12. Bonnie Angelo and Toni Morrison, "The Pain of Being Black," *Time*, May 22, 1989, 122.

13. Aida Mallard, "Homicide Is Leading Cause of Death of Black Males Age 44 and Younger in the U.S.," *Gainesville Sun*, June 17, 2020.

14. For the crucial term *slow death*, see Lauren Berlant, *Cruel Optimism* (Durham, NC: Duke University Press, 2011). For the HIV/AIDS statistics I cite, see "HIV: African Americans," CDC, accessed December 1, 2020, https://www.cdc.gov/hiv/group/racialethnic/africanamericans/index.html.

15. See Lisa Lowe, *Immigrant Acts: On Asian American Cultural Politics* (Durham, NC: Duke University Press, 1996).

16. "Page Act of 1875," Wikipedia, accessed October 14, 2020, https://en.wikipedia.org/wiki/Page_Act_of_1875.

17. Lisa Lowe, "Immigrant Acts," in *Intersectionality: Foundations and Frontiers*, 2nd ed., ed. Patrick R. Grzanka (New York: Routledge, 2019), 40.

18. "Chinese Exclusion Act," Wikipedia, accessed November 14, 2020, https://en.wikipedia.org/wiki/Chinese_Exclusion_Act#:~:text=The%20Chinese%20Exclusion%20Act%20was,all%20immigration%20of%20Chinese%20laborers.

19. Quoted in David L. Eng, *Racial Castration: Managing Masculinity in Asian America* (Durham, NC: Duke University Press, 2001), 138. Subsequent quotations from this section are from page 138.

20. For a book that reminds us that Native peoples' slavery is also a critical piece of this history, see Alan Gallay, *The Indian Slave Trade: The Rise of the English Empire in the American South, 1670–1717* (New Haven, CT: Yale University Press, 2002).

21. For a crucial book whose title says it all, see David Wallace Adams, *Education for Extinction: American Indians and the Boarding School Experience, 1875–1928*, 3rd ed. (Lawrence: University of Kansas Press, 1995).

22. Luther Standing Bear, *Land of the Spotted Eagle*, new ed. (Lincoln, Nebraska: Bison Books, 2006).

23. Mark Rifkin, *When Did Indians Become Straight? Kinship, the History of Sexuality, and Native Sovereignty* (New York: Oxford University Press, 2011), 8. In a footnote to his statement, Rifkin adds: "While playfully invoking 'straight'-ness, what I am really speaking about here is a system of heteronormativity, which is not equivalent to the privileging of heterosexual object choice, as I discuss later."

24. See Mary Zaborskis, "Sexual Orphanings," *GLQ: A Journal of Lesbian and Gay Studies* 22, no. 4 (2016): 605–628. Zaborskis, unlike Rifkin, *is* pointedly speaking to object choice, along with the broader parameters of heteronormativity that Rifkin explores.

25. Joshua Whitehead, *full-metal indigiqueer* (Vancouver: Talonbooks, 2017), back cover. See also Joshua Whitehead, *Jonny Appleseed* (Vancouver: Arsenal Pulp Press, 2018).

26. Qwo-Li Driskill, *Asegi Stories: Cherokee Queer and Two-Spirit Memory* (Tucson: University of Arizona Press, 2016), 5. The next two quotations are from pages 5 and 3, respectively.

27. Linda Tuhiwai Smith, *Decolonizing Methodologies: Research and Indigenous Peoples* (New York: Zed Books, 1999), 13.

28. Driskill, *Asegi Stories*, 23 and 5. Subsequent quotations in this section are from 4, 10–11, 13, 13, 13, 13, 13, 39, 55, 67, 64, 46, 48, 105, 109, 110, 112.

Chapter 4

1. Cady Lang, "Billy Porter Wore a Uterus Motif to the Tony Awards to Make a Statement," *Time*, June 10, 2019, https://time.com/5603960/billy porter tonys 2019 red carpet/.

2. Quoted in Shea Simmons, "Billy Porter's 2019 Oscars Tuxedo Gown Gave Him Power He Didn't Know He Had," *Bustle*, January 9, 2020, https://www.bustle.com/p/billy-porters-2019-oscars-tuxedo-gown-gave-him-power-he-didnt-know-he-had-19780882.

3. Mari Uyehara, "The Righteous Arrival of Megan Rapinoe," *GQ*, November 25, 2019, 120. Subsequent quotations in this section are found on page 121.

4. Jacqueline Rose, *Sexuality in the Field of Vision* (London: Verso Press, 1986), 90–91.

5. Sigmund Freud, "Femininity," *New Introductory Lectures on Psychoanalysis*, trans. and ed. James Strachey, Lecture 33 (New York: Norton, 1965), 132. All further references to Freud are from the same page.

6. If Billy Porter has his uterus dress, Janelle Monáe has rocked her vagina pants. See Callie Ahlgrim, "Janelle Monáe's Performance at the Grammys Was a Tribute to Vaginas and People Were Here for It," *Insider*, February 10, 2019, https://www.insider.com/grammys-janelle-monae-performance-vagina-monologue-pants-2019-2. This was definitely an instance of wearing your genitals on your clothes.

7. See "Coca Cola Super Bowl Commercial 2018 The Wonder of Us," YouTube, February 1, 2018, https://www.youtube.com/watch?v=-R-EEdvDrUU.

8. Malcolm Gladwell, "Listening to Khakis: What America's Most Popular Pants Tell Us about the Way Guys Think," *New Yorker,* July 28, 1997, 56. Subsequent quotations from Gladwell in this section are from pages 57, 62.

9. I focus on the original *Queer Eye* to get at these dynamics most pointedly. The newest *Queer Eye* (starting in 2018), which has dropped the phrase "for the straight guy," has broadened its appeal by doing makeovers for a whole range of people beyond straight men. Watching these two *Queer Eyes*, back to back, shows fascinating indications of change. It also shows traces of the rehearsal of failure I am noting here.

10. Michael Brick, "Guy in Skirt Seeks Sensitivity in Brooklyn," *New York Times,* November 2, 2003, section 9, page 1.

11. Watch TV for a day—newscasters, weathermen, sports announcers—and you'll see what I mean. Watches are bold, shoes are glamorous (with carefully chosen socks), and even the plumpest of men are sporting highly tailored suits with top button fastened, bottom button open. For an indication of freer experiments, see this article on Harry Styles: Orla Pentelow, "Harry Styles' *Vogue* Covers Is the Stuff of Dreams," *Bustle*, November 13, 2020, https://www.bustle.com/style/harry-styles-vogue-joy-in-playing-with-clothes-breaking-barriers. There it's said: "From kilts to Gucci gowns, Styles epitomises a new generation of ahem, style, devoid of any traces of toxic masculinity, and, of course, nails each and every one of the looks."

12. I've had much to say on this: see Stockton, *Making Out*, 21–30.

13. See this post on the website for the National Center for Transgender Equality: "Murders of Transgender People in 2020 Surpasses Total for Last Year in Just Seven Months," August 7, 2020, https://transequality.org/blog/murders-of-transgender-people-in-2020-surpasses-total-for-last-year-in-just-seven-months. There we are specifically told: "At least 28 transgender people have been murdered, or their death is suspicious, so far this year compared

to 26 last year. According to data collected by the National Center for Transgender Equality, 23 of the victims were transgender women, four were transgender men and one was non-binary. The epidemic of violence is particularly pronounced for Black and Latina trans women."

14. I don't mean that I wouldn't know how to tell the story of antiBlack racism for this period. I wouldn't know how to narrate the changing relation to *skin*, quite specifically. In contrast to clothing, we can't see people making different skin "choices," to put the matter awkwardly.

15. Eli Clare, *Brilliant Imperfection: Grappling with Cure* (Durham, NC: Duke University Press, 2017), 5. Subsequent quotations from Clare in this section are from pages 5, 5, 6, 6, 37, 38, 8–9.

16. Matthew Reeve, Ian A. Hunt, and Stuart Watts, dir., *Christopher Reeve: Hope in Motion* (Newtown, PA: Virgil Films, 2007).

17. Clare, *Brilliant Imperfection*, 11. Subsequent quotations are from pages 11, 11, 137, 137, 138, 140, 138, 19, 17.

18. See Clare, 140–142, for his wonderful elaboration of these changing categories. To put some of this in a (large) nutshell: the first edition of the *Diagnostic and Statistical Manual* (1952), published by the American Psychological Association, includes "transvestism" as a type of "Sexual Deviation." Other deviations from that time include "homosexuality, pedophilia, fetishism, and sexual sadism (including rape, sexual assault, and mutilation)" (38–39). The third edition of the *DSM* (1980) lists "transvestic fetishism" under "Paraphilias." The *DSM III-R* launches "Gender Identity Disorders," a category of disorders that includes "gender identity disorder of childhood" (302:60), "transsexualism" (302:50), and "gender identity disorder of adolescence or adulthood, nontranssexual type" (302:85). In 2013, the editors of the *DSM-V* came to the realization that for individuals "with conflicting or ambiguous biological indicators of sex (i.e., 'intersex'), the lived role in society and/or the identification as male or female could not be uniformly associated with or predicted from the biological indicators, and later that some individuals develop an identity as female or male at variance with their uniform set of classical biological indicators" (451). Thus, the *DSM-V* concludes: "gender dysphoria refers to the distress that may accompany the incongruence between one's experience or expressed gender and one's assigned gender" (451).

19. Jasbir Puar, *The Right to Maim: Debility, Capacity, Disability* (Durham, NC: Duke University Press, 2017), xiv. The full phrase in Puar is "the slow wearing down of populations instead of the event of becoming disabled." See also Rob Nixon, *Slow Violence and the Environmentalism of the Poor* (Cambridge, MA: Harvard University Press, 2011); and Elizabeth Povinelli, *Economies of*

Abandonment: Social Belonging and Endurance in Late Liberalism (Durham, NC: Duke University Press, 2011).

20. One statement—from 1968—profoundly captures what I am calling, informed by Puar, the "debilitating arm of the law": aspects of the legal system that actually *seek* to debilitate certain populations. This bold admission from the "Law and Order" White House of President Nixon was made by John Ehrlichman, Nixon's top advisor: "The Nixon White House . . . had two enemies: the antiwar left and black people. . . . We knew we couldn't make it illegal to be either against the war or black . . . but by getting the public to associate the hippies with marijuana and blacks with heroin, and then criminalizing both heavily, we could disrupt those communities. . . . We could arrest their leaders, raid their homes, break up their meetings, and vilify them night after night on the evening news. Did we know we were lying about the drugs? Of course we did" (quoted in the documentary *13th*, dir. Eva DuVernay [Netflix, 2016]).

21. See: "Herstory," Black Lives Matter, accessed October 19, 2020, https://blacklivesmatter.com/herstory/.

22. Christopher Flavelle, "Climate Change Tied to Pregnancy Risks, Affecting Black Mothers Most," *New York Times*, June 18, 2020, https://www.nytimes.com/2020/06/18/climate/climate-change-pregnancy-study.html.

Glossary

1. "Non-Binary Gender," Wikipedia, accessed October 20, 2020, https://en.wikipedia.org/wiki/Non-binary_gender.

2. Ruth Wilson Gilmore, *Golden Gulag: Prisons, Surplus, Crisis, and Opposition in Globalizing California* (Berkeley: University of California Press, 2007), 247.

BIBLIOGRAPHY

Adams, David Wallace. *Education for Extinction: American Indians and the Boarding School Experience, 1875–1928*. 3rd ed. Lawrence: University of Kansas Press, 1995.

Ahlgrim, Callie. "Janelle Monáe's Performance at the Grammys Was a Tribute to Vaginas and People Were Here for It." *Insider,* February 10, 2019. https://www.insider.com/grammys-janelle-monae-performance-vagina-monologue-pants-2019-2.

Angelides, Steven. *The Fear of Child Sexuality: Young People, Sex, and Agency*. Chicago: University of Chicago Press, 2019.

Angelo, Bonnie, and Toni Morrison. "The Pain of Being Black." *Time,* May 22, 1989.

Bailey, Marlon M. *Butch Queens Up in Pumps: Gender, Performance, and Ballroom Culture in Detroit*. Ann Arbor: University of Michigan Press, 2013.

Belleau, Marie-Claire. "L'intersectionalité: Feminisms in a Divided World." In *Feminist Politics: Identity, Difference, Agency*, edited by Deborah Orr, Dianna Taylor, Eileen Kahl, Kathleen Earle, Christa Rainwater, and Linda López McAlister, 51–62. Lanham, MD: Rowman & Littlefield, 2007.

Berlant, Lauren. *Cruel Optimism*. Durham, NC: Duke University Press, 2011.

Bernstein, Robin. *Racial Innocence: Performing American Childhood from Slavery to Civil Rights*. New York: New York University Press, 2011.

"Black and White in America." *Newsweek,* March 7, 1988. https://www.ebay.com/itm/NEWSWEEK-Magazine-March-7-1988-Black-White-Integrated-America-Winter-Olympics-/333683344949.

Brick, Michael. "Guy in Skirt Seeks Sensitivity in Brooklyn." *New York Times,* November 2, 2003, section 9, page 1.

Brooks, David. "The Culture of Policing Is Broken." *Atlantic,* June 16, 2020. https://www.theatlantic.com/ideas/archive/2020/06/how-police-brutality-gets-made/613030/.

Chávez, Karma R. *Queer Migration Politics: Activist Rhetoric and Coalitional Possibilities*. Urbana: University of Illinois Press, 2013.

Chow, Andrew R. "Old Town, New Road: How 20-Year-Old Upstart Lil Nas X Used the Internet to Beat Nashville at Its Own Game." *Time*, August 26, 2019.

Cisneros, Jesus. "Undocuqueer: Beyond the Shadows and the Closet." In *Intersectionality: Foundations and Frontiers*, 2nd ed., edited by Patrick R. Grzanka, 322–329. New York: Routledge, 2019.

Clare, Eli. *Brilliant Imperfection: Grappling with Cure*. Durham, NC: Duke University Press, 2017.

Cleaver, Eldridge. *Soul on Ice*. New York: Dell, 1968.

Cobb, Michael. *Single: Arguments for the Uncoupled*. New York: New York University Press, 2012.

Collins, Patricia Hill. *Black Feminist Thought: Knowledge, Consciousness and the Politics of Empowerment*. London: Hyman, 1990.

Crenshaw, Kimberlé Williams. "Demarginalizing the Intersection of Race and Sex: A Black Feminist Critique of Antidiscrimination Doctrine, Feminist Theory, and Antiracist Politics." *Chicago Legal Forum* (1989): 139–168.

Crenshaw, Kimberlé Williams. "The Structural and Political Dimensions of Intersectional Oppression." In *Intersectionality: Foundations and Frontiers*, 2nd ed., edited by Patrick R. Grzanka, 42–48. New York: Routledge, 2019.

Dockterman, Eliana. "A Doll for Everyone." In "The Science of Gender," special issue, *Time*. New York: Meredith Corporation, 2020.

Driskill, Qwo-Li. *Asegi Stories: Cherokee Queer and Two-Spirit Memory*. Tucson: University of Arizona Press, 2016.

DuVernay, Eva, dir. *13th*. Netflix, 2016.

Eng, David L. *Racial Castration: Managing Masculinity in Asian America*. Durham, NC: Duke University Press, 2001.

Fausto-Sterling, Anne. *Sex/Gender: Biology in a Social World*. New York: Routledge, 2012.

Fincher, David, dir. *Fight Club*. Los Angeles: 20th Century Fox, 1999.

Flavelle, Christopher. "Climate Change Tied to Pregnancy Risks, Affecting Black Mothers Most." *New York Times*, June 18, 2020. https://www.nytimes.com/2020/06/18/climate/climate-change-pregnancy-study.html.

Foner, Philip S. *Organized Labor and the Black Worker, 1619–1981*. 2nd ed. New York: International Publishers, 1982.

Foucault, Michel. *Discipline and Punish: The Birth of the Prison*. Translated by Alan Sheridan. New York: Vintage, 1979.

Freud, Sigmund. "Femininity." In *New Introductory Lectures on Psychoanalysis*, translated and edited by James Strachey. Lecture 33. New York: Norton, 1965.

Friedman, Claire. "The Electable Female Candidate." *New Yorker*, December 16, 2019.

Gallay, Alan. *The Indian Slave Trade: The Rise of the English Empire in the American South, 1670–1717*. New Haven, CT: Yale University Press, 2002.

Geary, Daniel. "The Moynihan Report." *Atlantic*, September 14, 2015. https://www.theatlantic.com/politics/archive/2015/09/the-moynihan-report-an-annotated-edition/404632/.

Gilchrist, Tracy E. "One Million Moms: Mattel's Gender-Inclusive Dolls Promote 'Sin.'" *ADVOCATE*, October 2, 2019. https://www.advocate.com/business/2019/10/02/one-millions-moms-mattels-gender-inclusive-dolls-promote-sin.

Gill-Peterson, Jules. *Histories of the Transgender Child*. Minneapolis: University of Minnesota Press, 2018.

Gilmore, Ruth Wilson. *Golden Gulag: Prisons, Surplus, Crisis, and Opposition in Globalizing California*. Berkeley: University of California Press, 2007.

Gladwell, Malcolm. "Listening to Khakis: What America's Most Popular Pants Tell Us about the Way Guys Think." *New Yorker*, July 28, 1997, 54–65.

Grzanka, Patrick R. "Intersectional Objectivity: On Knowledge and Violence." In *Intersectionality: Foundations and Frontiers*, 2nd ed., ed. Patrick R. Grzanka, 1–24. New York: Routledge, 2019.

Guy-Sheftall, Beverly, ed. *Words of Fire: An Anthology of African-American Feminist Thought*. New York: Norton, 1995.

Halberstam, Jack. *Trans*: A Quick and Quirky Account of Gender Variability*. Oakland: University of California Press, 2018.

Harzewski, Stephanie. *Chick Lit and Postfeminism*. Charlottesville: University of Virginia Press, 2011.

Heid, Markham. "Biology and the Brain." In "The Science of Gender," special issue, *Time*. New York: Meredith Corporation, 2020.

Horton, Alex. "'The Military's #MeToo': Vanessa Guillén's Slaying Has Many Servicewomen Revisiting Their Own Deep Scars." *Washington Post*, July 7, 2020. https://www.washingtonpost.com/national-security/2020/07/07/vanessa -guillen-servicewomen-veterans/.

Irigaray, Luce. *This Sex Which Is Not One*. Translated by Catherine Porter with Carolyn Burke. Ithaca, NY: Cornell University Press, 1985.

Jordan-Young, Rebecca M., and Katrina Karkazis. *Testosterone: An Unauthorized Biography*. Cambridge, MA: Harvard University Press, 2019.

Karkazis, Katrina. *Fixing Sex: Intersex, Medical Authority, and Lived Experience*. Durham, NC: Duke University Press, 2008.

Kluger, Jeffrey. "Not That Different from One Another." In "The Science of Gender," special issue, *Time*. New York: Meredith Corporation, 2020.

Kogan, Terry. "Sex-Separated Restrooms: An Exploration in Architecture, Gender & Law." Unpublished manuscript, consulted on June 16, 2020.

Lang, Cady. "Billy Porter Wore a Uterus Motif to the Tony Awards to Make a Statement." *Time*, June 10, 2019. https://time.com/5603960/billy-porter -tonys-2019-red-carpet/.

Lazzaro, Sage. "Tinder Just Became Trans and Non-Conforming Inclusive with 37 New Gender Options." *Observer*, November 15, 2016. https://observer .com/2016/11/tinder-just-became-trans-and-non-conforming-inclusive-with -37-new-gender-options/.

Lim, Eng-Beng. *Brown Boys and Rice Queens: Spellbinding Performance in the Asias*. New York: New York University Press, 2014.

Lowe, Lisa. "Immigrant Acts." In *Intersectionality: Foundations and Frontiers*, 2nd ed., edited by Patrick R. Grzanka, 36–41. New York: Routledge, 2019.

Lowe, Lisa. *Immigrant Acts: On Asian American Cultural Politics*. Durham, NC: Duke University Press, 1996.

Mallard, Aida. "Homicide Is Leading Cause of Death of Black Males Age 44 and Younger in the U.S." *Gainesville Sun*, June 17, 2020.

Martin, Jonathan. *World War I in Color*. Silver Spring, MD: Acorn Media, 2010. DVD.

Milian, Claudia. *LatinX*. Minneapolis: University of Minnesota Press, 2020.

Moore, Terry. "Why Is 'X' the Unknown?" TED Talk, February 2012. https://www.ted.com/talks/terry_moore_why_is_x_the_unknown?language=en.

Moraga, Cherríe. *Loving in the War Years: Lo que nunca pasó por sus labios*. Cambridge, MA: South End Press, 2000.

Moreau, Julie. "Year after Trans Military Ban, Legal Battle Rages On." OUT Politics and Policy, NBC News, April 11, 2020. https://www.nbcnews.com/feature/nbc-out/year-after-trans-military-ban-legal-battle-rages-n1181906.

Nixon, Rob. *Slow Violence and the Environmentalism of the Poor*. Cambridge, MA: Harvard University Press, 2011.

Nolan, Ian T., Christopher J. Kuhner, and Geolani W. Dy. "Demographic and Temporal Trends in Transgender Identities and Gender Confirming Surgery." *Translational Andrology and Urology* 8, no. 3 (June 2019): 184–190. https://doi.org/10.21037/tau.2019.04.09

Orenstein, Peggy. *Boys & Sex*. New York: Harper Collins, 2020.

Orenstein, Peggy. "The Miseducation of the American Boy: Why Boys Crack Up at Rape 'Jokes,' Think Having a Girlfriend Is 'Gay,' and Still Can't Cry—and Why We Need to Give Them New and Better Models of Masculinity." *Atlantic*, January/February 2020.

Orenstein, Peggy. "Peggy Orenstein on 'Boys & Sex.'" Interview by Doug Fabrizio. Radiowest, January 24, 2020. https://radiowest.kuer.org/post/peggy-orenstein-boys-sex.

Pentelow, Orla. "Harry Styles' *Vogue* Covers Is the Stuff of Dreams." *Bustle*, November 13, 2020. https://www.bustle.com/style/harry-styles-vogue-joy-in-playing-with-clothes-breaking-barriers.

Plato. *The Symposium*. Translated by Walter Hamilton. New York: Penguin, 1951.

Povinelli, Elizabeth. *Economies of Abandonment: Social Belonging and Endurance in Late Liberalism*. Durham, NC: Duke University Press, 2011.

Puar, Jasbir K. *The Right to Maim: Debility, Capacity, Disability*. Durham, NC: Duke University Press, 2017.

Randall, Alice. *The Wind Done Gone*. New York: Mariner, 2002.

Ransby, Barbara. *Making All Black Lives Matter*. Berkeley: University of California Press, 2018.

Reeve, Matthew, Ian A. Hunt, and Stuart Watts, dir. *Christopher Reeve: Hope in Motion*. Newtown, PA: Virgil Films, 2007.

Rifkin, Mark. *When Did Indians Become Straight? Kinship, the History of Sexuality, and Native Sovereignty*. New York: Oxford University Press, 2011.

Rodríguez, Juana María. *Sexual Futures, Queer Gestures, and Other Latina Longings*. New York: New York University Press, 2014.

Rose, Jacqueline. *Sexuality in the Field of Vision*. London: Verso Press, 1986.

Rubin, Gayle. "The Traffic in Women: Notes on the 'Political Economy' of Sex." In *The Second Wave: A Reader in Feminist Theory*, edited by Linda Nicholson, 27–62. New York: Routledge, 1997.

Saketopolou, Avgi. "Risking Sexuality Beyond Consent: Overwhelm and the Suffering of Pleasure in Jeremy O. Harris's *Slave Play*." Unpublished manuscript, consulted on July 12, 2020.

Sengupta, Shuddhabrata. "Identity as a Weapon of Mass Destruction." In *Intersectionality: Foundations and Frontiers*, 2nd ed., edited by Patrick R. Grzanka, 118–123. New York: Routledge, 2019.

Simmons, Shea. "Billy Porter's 2019 Oscars Tuxedo Gown Gave Him Power He Didn't Know He Had." *Bustle*, January 9, 2020. https://www.bustle.com/p /billy-porters-2019-oscars-tuxedo-gown-gave-him-power-he-didnt-know-he -had-19780882.

Smith, Barbara. "Doing It from Scratch: The Challenge of Black Lesbian Organizing." In *The Truth that Never Hurts: Writings on Race, Gender and Freedom*, edited by Barbara Smith, 167–177. New Brunswick, NJ: Rutgers University Press, 1998.

Smith, Barbara. "Racism and Women's Studies." In *Intersectionality: Foundations and Frontiers*, 2nd ed., edited by Patrick R. Grzanka, 63–66. New York: Routledge, 2019.

Smith, Linda Tuhiwai. *Decolonizing Methodologies: Research and Indigenous Peoples*. New York: Zed Books, 1999.

Snorton, C. Riley. *Black on Both Sides: A Racial History of Trans Identity*. Minneapolis: University of Minnesota Press, 2017.

Spillers, Hortense J. "Mama's Baby, Papa's Maybe: An American Grammar Book." *Diacritics* 17 (Summer 1987): 64–81.

Standing Bear, Luther. *Land of the Spotted Eagle*. New ed. Lincoln, Nebraska: Bison Books, 2006.

Stockton, Kathryn Bond. *Beautiful Bottom, Beautiful Shame: Where "Black" Meets "Queer."* Durham, NC: Duke University Press, 2006.

Stockton, Kathryn Bond. *Making Out*. New York: New York University Press, 2019.

Stockton, Kathryn Bond. *The Queer Child, or Growing Sideways in the Twentieth Century*. Durham, NC: Duke University Press, 2009.

Sullivan, Andrew. "The He Hormone." *New York Times Magazine*, April 2, 2000.

Taylor, Keeanga-Yamahtta, ed. *How We Get Free: Black Feminism and the Combahee River Collective*. Chicago: Haymarket Books, 2017.

Urquhart, Evan. "The Lie Hormone." *Slate*, January 22, 2018. https://slate.com/human-interest/2018/01/andrew-sullivans-ode-to-testosterone-is-rooted-is-stereotypes.html.

Uyehara, Mari. "The Righteous Arrival of Megan Rapinoe." *GQ*, November 25, 2019.

Vrangalova, Zhana. "Research Shows Many Trans Folks' Sexual Attractions Change after Transition." *them.*, June 25, 2018. https://www.them.us/story/sexual-attraction-after-transition.

Whitehead, Joshua. *full-metal indigiqueer.* Vancouver: Talonbooks, 2017.

Whitehead, Joshua. *Jonny Appleseed.* Vancouver: Arsenal Pulp Press, 2018.

Zaborskis, Mary. "Sexual Orphanings." *GLQ: A Journal of Lesbian and Gay Studies* 22, no. 4 (2016): 605–628.

Zaveri, Mihir. "Virginia Schools' Bathroom Rule Violates Transgender Rights, U.S. Judge Says." *New York Times,* August 9, 2019. https://www.nytimes.com /2019/08/09/us/virginia-transgender-bathroom-policy.html.

FURTHER READING

Bergner, Daniel. "Neither/Nor." *New York Times Magazine*, June 9, 2019, 36–45.

Bornstein, Kate. *Gender Outlaw: On Men, Women, and the Rest of Us*. Revised and updated ed. New York: Vintage, 2016.

Butler, Judith. *Gender Trouble*. New York: Routledge, 1990.

DeLisle, Christine Taitano. *Placental Politics: CHamoru Women, White Womanhood, and Indigeneity under U.S. Colonialism in Guam*. Chapel Hill: University of North Carolina Press, forthcoming.

Diamond, Lisa. *Sexual Fluidity: Understanding Women's Love and Desire*. Cambridge, MA: Harvard University Press, 2008.

Driskill, Qwo-Li, Chris Finley, Brian Joseph Gilley, and Scott Lauria Morgensen, eds. *Queer Indigenous Studies: Critical Interventions in Theory, Politics, and Literature*. Tucson: University of Arizona Press, 2011.

Gopinath, Gayatri. *Impossible Desires: Queer Diasporas and South Asian Public Cultures*. Durham, NC: Duke University Press, 2005.

Hammonds, Evelyn, and Rebecca M. Herzig. *The Nature of Difference: Sciences of Race in the United States from Jefferson to Genomics*. Cambridge, MA: MIT Press, 2009.

Hartman, Saidiya. *Wayward Lives, Beautiful Experiments: Intimate Histories of Riotous Black Girls, Troublesome Women, and Queer Radicals*. New York: Norton, 2019.

Johnson, E. Patrick. *Sweet Tea: Black Gay Men of the South*. Chapel Hill: University of North Carolina Press, 2008.

Jolly, Margaret. "Moving Masculinities: Memories and Bodies Across Oceania." In "Remembering Oceanic Masculinities," special issue, *Contemporary Pacific* 20, no. 1 (2008): 1–24.

Jordan-Young, Rebecca. *Brain Storm: The Flaws in the Science of Sex Differences*. Cambridge, MA: Harvard University Press, 2011.

Kafer, Alison. *Feminist, Queer, Crip*. Bloomington: Indiana University Press, 2013.

Kim, Eunjung. *Curative Violence: Rehabilitating Disability, Gender, and Sexuality in Modern Korea*. Durham, NC: Duke University Press, 2016.

Lee, Rachel C. *The Exquisite Corpse of Asian America: Biopolitics, Biosociality, and Posthuman Ecologies*. New York: New York University Press, 2014.

Lima, Lázaro. *Being Brown: Sonia Sotomayor and the Latino Question*. Oakland: University of California Press, 2019.

Lorde, Audre. *Sister Outsider*. New York: Crossing Press, 1984.

Marriott, David. *On Black Men*. New York: Columbia University Press, 2000.

McKittrick, Katherine, ed. *Sylvia Wynter: On Being Human as Praxis*. Durham, NC: Duke University Press, 2015.

Mock, Janet. *Redefining Realness: My Path to Womanhood, Identity, Love & So Much More*. New York: Atria Books, 2014.

Muñoz, José Esteban. *Disidentifications: Queers of Color and the Politics of Performance*. Minneapolis: University of Minnesota Press, 1999.

Musser, Amber. *Sensual Excess: Queer Femininity and Brown Jouissance*. New York: New York University Press, 2018.

Perry, Imani. *Vexy Thing: On Gender and Liberation*. Durham, NC: Duke University Press, 2018.

Reeser, Todd W. *Masculinities in Theory: An Introduction*. Malden, MA: Blackwell, 2010.

Teves, Stephanie Nohelani. *Defiant Indigeneity: The Politics of Hawaiian Performance.* Chapel Hill: University of North Carolina Press, 2018.

slow death and, 153, 192–194
Two-Spirit, 161–166
Near the Big Chakra, 109
Nonbinaryness, 2, 16, 19, 27–29, 35,
    172, 179, 182, 184
North Carolina's HB 2, 141

Obama, Barack, 20, 123
Orenstein, Peggy, 61–71, 73–74,
    105, 110, 172–173, 189

Page Act of 1875, 154–155
Parents. *See* Gender/sex, parents and
Plato, 133–136
Porter, Billy, 6, 169–170, 172, 174
Pratt, Richard Henry, 158–161
Pronouns. *See* Gender/sex,
    pronouns
Psychoanalysis, 110–114, 172.
    See also Freud, Sigmund;
    Unconscious, the

Queer, 37. *See also* Asian (American)
    people; Black Americans;
    Gender/sex; Latinas/Latinos/
    Chicanas/Chicanos and brown
    racialization; Native Americans;
    Race; Sexuality; Transgender
  bisexual identities, 81–82, 162
  closeting/coming out, 33–34, 76–
    83, 123–128, 156–157
  concepts of opposite sex, 11–12,
    107–108, 133–138, 145–150,
    154–166
  concepts of same sex, 38–39, 107,
    132, 135–137, 144–151
  gay identities/issues, 21, 32–34,
    36–37, 67, 76–85, 124–125, 162,
    176–178, 183–184

"heterosexuality," 67, 73–74, 107–
    108, 122, 132–136, 145–149,
    153, 157, 161
"homosexuality," 38, 66–68, 132–
    137, 146–147, 149, 158
  lesbian identities/issues, 67, 85,
    109, 114–120, 126–128, 137,
    162, 184
  LGBT identities, 37, 123–126,
    162
  straight identities/issues, 41, 70–
    75, 80, 156, 175–178, 183–184
  straightness as, 11, 36–37, 70–75,
    156–157, 161, 175–178, 179
  as strange, 11, 19, 36–40, 70–75,
    105, 148, 161–166, 184
  undocuqueer and migration issues,
    123–128
*Queer Eye/Queer Eye for the Straight
    Guy*, 84, 178–179

Race. *See also* Asian (American)
    people; Black Americans;
    Class; Gender/sex; Genitals;
    Indigeneity; Latinas/Latinos/
    Chicanas/Chicanos and brown
    racialization; Money; Native
    Americans; White Americans
    and whiteness
  assigned at birth, 3, 41, 205n1
  "biology" and, 54–55, 59–60, 119,
    146
  cities and, 77–78
  colonialism/postcolonialism,
    86–91
  environmental (anti)racism,
    193–196
  migration issues and, 85–86, 93,
    123–128

military ban in US, 19–22
    race and, 96–97
    women's colleges and, 27–29
Trump, Donald, 20–22
Tubman, Harriet, 115
Two-Spirit. *See* Native Americans,
    Two-Spirit

Unconscious, the, 45–46, 52, 167,
    172, 175, 182–183
Urquhart, Evan, 51, 57–58

Van Ness, Jonathan, 84

White Americans and whiteness. *See
    also* Gender/sex; Queer; Race
    categories of men/women and
        masculine/feminine, 12, 25, 37–
        38, 54–55, 63, 68, 70, 131–132
    Chicana lesbianism and, 127–128
    cisgender-surface privilege, 183–
        186
    "colorblind" presumptions of, 76,
        114, 122, 153, 208n28
    feminist racial insensitivity/
        racism of, 119–120
    girls and Black dolls and, 18–19
    medicine's attention to white
        intersex and transgender
        children, 95–97
    men's clothing and, 177–178
    privileged skin surface of, 173–
        174
    sameness of, 37–39, 137–138,
        146–147
    white supremacy and, 149, 151,
        156–161, 165–166, 192–194
Whitehead, Joshua, 161–162, 166
Wilde, Oscar, 124

Woman. *See* Asian (American)
    people; Black Americans; Class;
    Femininity; Feminism; Gender/
    sex; Genitals; Latinas/Latinos/
    Chicanas/Chicanos and brown
    racialization; Masculinity;
    Money; Native Americans;
    Queer; White Americans and
    whiteness
Woolley, Catherine, 48

Zaborskis, Mary, 161

KATHRYN BOND STOCKTON is Distinguished Professor of English, former Associate Vice President for Equity and Diversity, and inaugural Dean of the School for Cultural and Social Transformation at the University of Utah, where she teaches queer theory, theories of race, and twentieth-century literature and film. Two of her books, *Beautiful Bottom, Beautiful Shame: Where "Black" Meets "Queer"* and *The Queer Child, or Growing Sideways in the Twentieth Century*, published by Duke University Press, were finalists for the Lambda Literary Award in LGBT Studies, and she has authored *God between Their Lips: Desire between Women in Irigaray, Brontë, and Eliot* (Stanford University Press). Her recent book, *Making Out* (New York University Press), was a 2020 finalist for the Next Generation Indie Book Award for Memoir. Stockton has received the Crompton-Noll Prize, awarded by the Modern Language Association, for the best essay in gay and lesbian studies and has taught at Cornell University's School of Criticism and Theory, where she led a seminar on "Sexuality and Childhood in a Global Frame." In 2013, she was awarded the Rosenblatt Prize for Excellence, the highest honor granted by the University of Utah.